KIDS: AN OWNER'S MANUAL

End Of The List Series

Book 4

Jane Martin, LPC

KIDS: AN OWNER'S MANUAL

EOL Series, Book 4

Jane Martin, LPC

Jane Martin

ISBN-13: 978-1530869688

www.JaneMartin.org

Dedicated To Lois Riskin, my mother,
who gave me the experience of being forever loved.

Table of Contents

KIDS: AN OWNER'S MANUAL

INTRODUCTION

Today's parents face a dilemma—we detest the authoritarian model, the "children should be seen and not heard" approach, the "do-it-because-I-said-so" response, the punishment and humiliation, the cold harsh loveless home environment that has been our legacy, so we vow never to go there. We vow to cherish and nourish our children with kindness. One fifth of us have had great difficulty getting pregnant in the first place so we recognize, all the more, the precious gift that our child is. We promise ourselves to do everything in our power to give our child the happiest life possible.

So as soon as our children can express their wishes we take it upon ourselves to fulfill each wish to the fullest extent possible. This becomes our focus. We ask our children, all day long "What do you want now?" "Is it OK with you if I do this?" "Which of these do you like?" - question after question, directing their attention constantly to focus on their inclinations, and then, by our response, conveying to them the dire importance of bringing those inclinations to fruition. Rarely does such a child encounter life situations that require her to defer to the needs of other people, or to ensure her future well-being by delaying gratification.

Indeed, in those infrequent situations where her whim is not fulfilled, she becomes frantic, mistaking her wants for needs, acting as if her life is threatened, and using all her God-given powers to attain her desire. This behavior we label "bratty."

Fast-forward ten years. To our horror, instead of the strong, confident, considerate, psychologically healthy teenager that we expect as the result of all our years of devoted, selfless parenting, we now have an undisciplined, out of control child, who seems unable to think past his own immediate desires, who has no care for his future or for the havoc he causes in other peoples' lives.

In fear, we crack down, a last desperate attempt to "discipline" the child, for his own good. But it is too late. A teenager is biologically programmed to attain autonomy, and all that results from this belated parenting effort is a huge battle of the wills.

This book essentially conveys one idea, that parents need to find a middle ground between "bootcamp" versus "mayhem" parenting, but conveys it deeply and thoroughly. I believe that if parents can understand this one idea, they will be able to avoid the troubles described above, and will be blessed with children who will possess what philosophers call "Inner Freedom"; an inner balance that, I contend, is a prerequisite for later spiritual growth. The book consists of a series of daily exercises, some of which require you to do something, others which are just reading material to digest. Each exercise will help you to understand and implement the basic idea.

I will look at physical causes of difficult behavior, discuss appropriate amounts of parental control at different ages, give a brief overview of the healthy development of the human psyche, and look at how different parenting methods affect this development. Hopefully, this will help you to decide when it is healthier for your child to say "yes" or "no" in any given situation. Then I will present my own system for effectively but lovingly saying no to young children, and resolving conflicts with older children. An exercise is provided to allow you to do your own inner work of releasing negative judgments against your children, so that your own negative feelings don't get in the way of helping your children. For those of you who know what to do, but often find yourself possessed by angry demons that yell at your kids, I describe the Buddhist method of transcending and releasing the grip of emotional reactions.

One of the additional benefits of finding that middle ground is that disciplining your child properly is essential to the healthy development of your child's prefrontal cortex (PFC). The PFC is the most highly evolved part of the brain and its dysfunction is associated with most mental health disorders. I give suggestions for 15 ways to raise a child with a healthy prefrontal cortex (PFC).

And lastly, for those with an interest in spiritual theory, I provide an explanation of why parenting in the way I describe forms the basis for later spiritual work.

This book is one part of an overall program called the End of the List Workshop (EOL). EOL is a series of daily 10 minute exercises designed to help you elevate your whole life. This book just concentrates on children, but the other books look at everything from your house to your emotions.

EOL works with 5 stages of elevating your life, and I will be referring to them throughout this book. They are:

Stage 1. Creating a clear vision of how you'd like this area of your life to be.

Stage 2. Learning relevant principles that relate to the area you'd like to elevate.

Stage 3. Brainstorming actions you can take to manifest your vision and make it a reality.

Stage 4. Putting each of those actions into practice, using a time system consisting of a schedule, a to do list, a calendar and a Morning Affirmation List.

Stage 5. Using contemplative review to examine whether your brainstormed ideas are working or need revision.

For more information on EOL and suggestions for creating a time system, see Appendix A.

STAGE 1

Creating a clear vision of how you'd like
your child's life to be.

Exercise One

CLEAR VISION CHECKLIST ONE

On the following pages is a checklist, to help you through Stage 1, creating a clear vision of how you'd like your children's lives to be. Don't try to do Stage 3, brainstorming, right now. During Stage 1 you will just make a list of things that you would like to change in any way. Don't try to think of *how* you want to accomplish this change just yet. You can do that later during Stage 3. Using the following checklists, just make a list right now of what you want to change, or problems that you see. Take your time and think deeply about your child. If you have more than one child, separate checklists are provided and you can repeat this exercise on subsequent days, one for each child.

Imagine this child before you. Describe her to yourself. Imagine how it feels to be her. Follow a typical day of hers in your mind, feeling her experience.

Right off the bat, before I list my questions, what is she saying to you? What does this child need? Think of her physical, intellectual, emotional and spiritual needs.

Now, going through the checklist, list any changes you want to make onto the Stage 1 checklist on the page 11.

A. PHYSICAL HEALTH

1. Does her body seem basically healthy and strong?

2. Does she have any chronic pains, no matter how small, persistent skin rashes or lumps or other even seemingly possibly insignificant, problems?

3. Is she substantially over or under weight?

4. Are her feet, legs, genitals, healthy and pain free? Are her periods healthy, her colon regular? How about her stomach, lungs, sinuses, joints, arms, hands, teeth, hair, toe and fingernails? Does she get headaches Or cold sores?

5. Does she need more rhythm - i.e. to wake and sleep at the same hour every day, eat meals and eliminate at the same time, etc.?

6. Does she need more exercise? How much would be ideal?

7. Does she get enough rest? Does she feel tired at the same time each day?

8. Is her diet close to your ideal of healthy? Would you benefit from some advice from a health care professional as to what would be best to eat? Does she eat compulsively, perhaps because of food addictions? What do you think of as an ideal diet? What do you think keeps her from eating this diet?

9. Do you think she needs to improve her appearance? Get a haircut? Buy new clothes? Or is she overly concerned with her appearance?

10. Is she doing unhealthy things?

B. SAFETY

11. Is your child safe?

12. Does he always wear a seatbelt, and a bike helmet?

13. Does he know what to do in case of fire, to drop and roll, how to get out the window, where your extinguishers are, and how to call 911?

14. Does your daughter *and your son* know that their body is their own and that it is wrong for a stranger or anyone to molest them or touch them in a way that makes them feel uncomfortable?

15. Do your little ones know what to do if they are separated from you in a crowd?

16. Do you go to a doctor or health care provider regularly? Get eye exams? (Be sure they are checked specifically for amblyopia.) Ear exams (I have friends in the deaf community and it's amazing how many didn't know their kids were deaf for years.)

17. Does your will clearly specify who will take your children in the event of your death?

C. BALANCE

18. Is your child's physical life balanced? Think of her weekly schedule.

19. Is there a balance between active and rest time?

20. Scheduled and free time?

21. Social and alone time?

22. Is there a balance between her needs and those of the people around her? Are you allowing her to fulfill her desires as long as it doesn't hurt her or anyone else or the environment? Conversely is she OK with sometimes foregoing her desires so as not to hurt herself, or anyone else?

STAGE ONE

Child's Name

_____

_____

_____

_____

_____

_____

_____

_____

_____

_____

_____

_____

_____

_____

_____

_____

_____

_____

Jane Martin

STAGE ONE

Child's Name

_____

_____

_____

_____

_____

_____

_____

_____

_____

_____

_____

_____

_____

_____

_____

STAGE ONE

Child's Name

_____

_____

_____

_____

_____

_____

_____

_____

_____

_____

_____

_____

_____

_____

_____

_____

Exercise Two

CLEAR VISION CHECKLIST TWO

As in the previous exercise, use this checklist to help you create your Stage 1 list, continuing to write on the previous pages, anything you'd like to work on changing.

A. INTELLECTUAL DEVELOPMENT

1. Does he do well in school?

2. Might he be better off in a public/private/homeschool environment?

3. Could he use extra help from a tutor or from you?

4. Does he feel comfortable asking you for help with his homework?

5. Is school providing enough stimulation for his developing mind?

6. Can you help him become interested in a hobby? What are his interests? My friend Shelly's grandma said the way to raise teenagers is to find their passion and support the heck out of it.

7. How much time does he spend watching TV and in front of the computer? Does this feel OK to you?

8. What is your child reading? Was it consciously chosen by you?

9. Does your child have the skills appropriate to his age? By the time he is 18, she/he should to be able to clean the house, cook all meals, sew, make appointments, be responsible about being on time, feel comfortable finding out information she/he doesn't know by

asking, or researching, have proper manners, be able to deal with his/her emotions, etc. YOU WONT ALWAYS BE THERE! Are you still pouring your five year old's milk? Is your eight year old doing regular chores? Kids need to feel that they are a significant part of the family. It benefits them to feel that they are capable of doing real worthwhile work, and to be a responsible member of a group. Society may have changed to the point where we no longer really need our children to chip in, but let's not deprive them of the positive aspects of this involvement. Write down some things you might like to work on.

B. EMOTIONAL DEVELOPMENT

Try to really feel this. Feel it in your stomach and your chest when you think of your child.

10. Is your child happy?

11. Is your child balanced emotionally?

12. Does she tend to be melancholic, whiney, to always focus on the down side? Can you think of ways to support her in letting things go, saying "It's OK," and counting her blessings, and having compassion for other more disadvantaged children? Perhaps expressing gratitude at meal time or before bed, saying a prayer for those in need? Cultivating the attitude that tomorrow is a new day.

13. Does this child tend to be volatile and overly emotional? To become angry, cry on a whim, or get out of control? Does she need clear boundaries, strong discipline, or more hugs and rocking chair time? Can you give her jobs where she is in charge or feels challenged?

14. Does he tend to be bratty? Do you accept speech and behavior from this child that makes you uncomfortable? If so, it would likely benefit him as well as you to not accept it. Do you feel you have problems disciplining your child and would benefit from a more conscious approach?

15. Does this child tend to be too slow and lazy? Do you find yourself practically having to scream to motivate her? Can you find ways to bring active, rhythmical activities into her life - running, biking, daily chores - in order to help develop her will?

16. Does this child tend too much toward superficiality, to talk nonstop, eat while hopping up and down, jump from one project to the next? Can you think of ways to help cultivate a deep love or passion for something? Can you insist on the completion of projects?

17. Does your child have high self-esteem?

18. Is she too arrogant?

19. Do you let your child know that your love is unconditional, that you accept him as he is, that she is a good, OK, person, who sometimes makes mistakes along the way. So what? We are all growing. Or is all she hears from you complaints about the mistakes that she does make?

20. Does your child do things that consistently annoy, anger, or worry you?

21. Do you have expectations of achievements for this child? Are you attached to them or are you open to letting the child blossom naturally in her own way?

22. Do you punish this child? Does it work? How do you feel in your gut about this? Have you considered alternatives?

C. SOCIAL DEVELOPMENT

23. How are the relationships in this child's life? With your spouse/partner, her grandparents, teachers, siblings, friends, strangers?

SPIRITUAL DEVELOPMENT

24. Do you want to include more outer form, rituals, acknowledgement of a higher power, in this child's life?

25. Now again, bring to your mind this child communicating to you with his/her whole being. What might he/she be saying to you?

For the next few days, go back to Exercise One and Two and make a Stage 1 list for each additional child. Hold on to these lists.

In the days following, we will learn some theory that will help you to do Stage 3, brainstorming actions for change, later on.

The way we parent our children affects their psychological well being, and on a brain level, this most prominently shows up in one section of the brain called the prefrontal cortex (PFC). The PFC sits right behind the forehead, and is the most highly evolved part of the brain. In the third section of this book I will list 15 parenting methods to support the healthy development of the PFC. The first method is discipline. Since most parents seek help around discipline theory, the next section of this book will address the subject of discipline.

STAGE 2

Learning Relevant Principles

Exercise Three

GOALS

"A mother is not a person to lean on but a person to make leaning unnecessary."
—Dorothy Canfield Fisher

Before we talk about how to discipline your children, we need to be sure that we have the same goals. I can help you to "get somewhere" with your children, but let's make sure that we are in agreement about where we want your children to get. This exercise will help you to become clear about your end goals for your child. Then with the next exercises, you will be able to see clearly how your discipline method is or is not helping you to attain these goals.

For this exercise, I suggest that you sit straight with your feet on the floor, and breathe fully, first into your belly, filling it like a balloon, and then into your chest. Then let the breath exhale on its own. Breathe 10 full breaths. Don't skip this part – it has an effect on your brain, shifting energy into your intuitive and feeling center, and away from your intellect. This will help you to tap into a deeper wisdom. After 10 breaths:

Imagine your child is walking out of the front door, suitcase in hand. He is 18 years old and is going off to college or out to live in the world, and turns to wave goodbye to you. You realize that you no longer have any control over him, and cannot be there every day to take care of him.

Make a list of the qualities and skills you would like this child to possess. For example you might list - cooking, doing the laundry, cleaning, shopping, and paying bills, being kind and considerate of others, being able to stand up for himself and taking care of his own needs.

QUALITIES AND SKILLS I WANT FOR MY GROWN CHILD

SKILLS NEEDED

(This column is filled
in with next exercise.)

_____   _____

_____   _____

_____   _____

_____   _____

_____   _____

_____   _____

_____   _____

_____   _____

_____   _____

_____   _____

_____   _____

_____   _____

_____   _____

_____   _____

Exercise Four

THE FOUR SKILLS

Below is a list of four skills that I believe your children must learn in order to attain your goals for them. The first two are about wants, and on their face they seem contradictory:

1. The ability to do what he wants. - To honor his own needs, and feel that he is worthy to fulfill his own desires. This requires that he be in touch with those desires.

2. The ability to NOT do what he wants. - This is the ability to do something he doesn't feel like doing, and the ability to refrain from doing something he feels like doing.

The second two skills are about deferring and also seem to be in conflict with each other:

3. The willingness to give over to others. - For example, to follow rules set out for the benefit of everyone, or to control his own inclination to make noise because it might wake someone up.

4. The willingness to NOT give over to others. - For example, if you think of the lives of the world's great achievers, you realize that they usually had to go against the "norm" and believe in themselves despite naysayers. The saying "Rules are for the obedience of fools, and the guidance of the wise" applies here. I like to call this the "Rosa Parks" skill.

The achievement of some of your goals for your child might require only one or two of these skills, but I'm sure that you will find that to achieve all your goals, your child must possess all four of these skills.

MATCHING THE 4 SKILLS WITH YOUR GOALS

Here is an exercise to help you become more fluent in understanding the 4 skills, and to allow you to see first hand how the attainment of these 4 skills will be necessary for your child to achieve the goals you have set for him.

For each of your goals that you listed in the previous exercise, note alongside it which of the 4 skills would be needed to attain that goal. Some goals will require more than one skill. Go ahead and do this exercise now. Then check what you have written against what others have written in workshops I have given, listed on the next page.

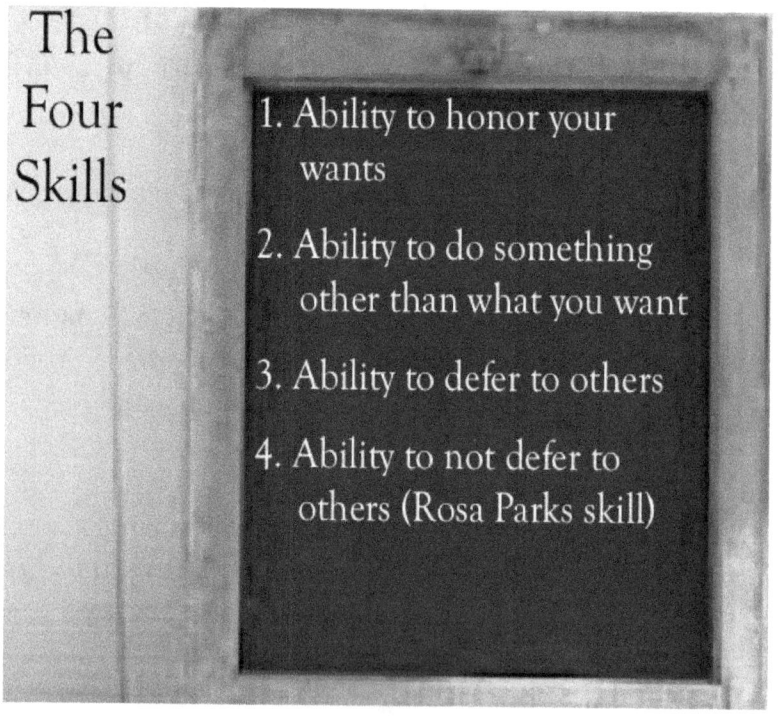

The
Four
Skills

1. Ability to honor your wants

2. Ability to do something other than what you want

3. Ability to defer to others

4. Ability to not defer to others (Rosa Parks skill)

Here is a list of goals that parents in my workshops have made, along with the corresponding skills they felt would be required.

Ability to make conscious choices 1, 2, 3, 4
Ability to manage time 2
Ability to set boundaries 1, 4
Be beyond cool (not be so affected by it) 4
Compassionate, kind, loving 3
Confidence 1, 4
Cooperative 3
Courage 2
Courage to be who they are even if it's different 1, 4
Creative and imaginative 1
Financially successful 1, 2, 3
Flexible 3
Good hugger 1
Happy 1, 2, 3, 4
Hardworking and persistent 2,4
Intelligent (none of the skills can help achieve this.)
Joy, Love of life 1
Independent and responsible 2, 4
Integrity and honest 1, 2, 3, 4
Love of God, within and without 1, 3
Moral 2, 3, 4
Organized 2
Peaceful 1, 2, 3, 4
Respectful to others 2, 3
Safe/know own limits 2
Self care skills – laundry, cooking, grooming etc 2
Self controlled 2
Self love, and esteem 1
Spiritual 1, 2, 3, 4
Unstoppable/Believing in his dreams 4

Exercise Five

THE BICYCLE ANALOGY

Many books about discipline fail to distinguish between children of different ages. This makes no sense to me! We will come back to work with the four skills in a bit. But first let's examine how the discipline needs of the child change as he grows older.

Here is a little puzzle, extremely simple to do, but it makes a very important point. I like to use the analogy of a bicycle. Suppose you have three kids. One is a toddler, one a school age kid, and the third a teenager. And suppose you have three bikes. One is a tricycle, one a bike with training wheels, and one a twelve-speed. It isn't difficult to see which bike is most appropriate for which kid, right?

Figure A

Here's the finished puzzle.

Figure B

Well, think of the bikes as representing differing levels of choice. The trike represents having very little choice. Your little toddler can lean all the way to the right, and all the way to the left, but that trike is still going to just sit there stable. The bike with training wheels permits some leaning to the left and right, but only within limits. This represents choice within limits. And the twelve-speed will totally fall over if the child decides to lean too far. This represents full choice.

It is as inappropriate to put a toddler on a twelve-speed, as it is to put a teen on a trike. These are the two discipline problems I see in our society. And it is my contention, that because we put our toddlers on twelve-speeds when they should be on tricycles (i.e. give them too much choice), they grow up to be teens who cannot negotiate the twelve-speed. At this point, the parents freak out and try to put the teen onto a trike. I will support this contention deeply with the upcoming discussion about the development of the child's psyche.

Properly parenting a toddler (putting him on a tricycle) sounds like this:

Good Morning!

Here is your breakfast.

Here are your clothes.

I have a client after nursery school today so you will be playing at Tommy's house.

Putting a toddler on a twelve-speed sounds like this:

Are you ready to wake up yet?

What would you like for breakfast? Cheerios, French toast, fruit salad, or granola? You want ice cream? Oh Gosh....

What would you like to wear? Your blue jeans, your purple dress, your green dress, ...

I have a client after school. Is it OK if you play with Tommy?

To check which kind of bike you are putting your toddler on, count the number of questions you ask him in an hour. Hmm..... If your child spends his day constantly consulting his own inclinations in order to answer your questions about what he wants, then he is a toddler on a twelve-speed.

A bike with training wheels (appropriate parenting for 7-12 year olds) sounds like this:

Good morning. Time to wake up.

I'm making French toast for breakfast. Want some, or would you like to make yourself some cereal?

Be sure to put on an outfit with a sweater, it's cold today.

I have a client after school, would you like to play with Tommy or Sally?

Trusting your teenager on a twelve-speed, where you move from authority to guidance, sounds like this:

Mom, we're going to stay up all night at Sally's sleepover!

Oh really? What might the consequences of that decision be?

Consequences? Oh... well, I guess I'll be tired the next day.

Probably. What do you have to do the next day?

Oh, I have my soccer tournament. Um, maybe I'll just stay up till 11:00.

Sounds wise.

If this parent were trying to put this teen on a trike, she might have answered:

No! You may not stay up all night.

And the teen might have answered:

&*&^(! I hate you, you are so mean.

So let's assume the worst-case scenario that the above teen does decide to stay up all night. What will happen? Maybe she won't do well at her soccer tournament. That's what it is to let go of the bike. You can't freak out if the bike falls now and then, as long as it falls on grass. It's all part of learning to ride, learning to live, learning to make good decisions. When she was one year old and learning to walk, you had to let go of her, even if she fell on her butt now and then. Of course, if she were near the stairway, you would take control back. Your teen needs practice, not to walk, but to make her own decisions. Isn't it nice to be there to put in your two cents while she learns? That's guidance.

Another example of empowering your teen:

Yo Dude! I see your wallet on the couch. Seems to me you've lost your wallet three times this week. What might you do to prevent that from happening again?

See how inappropriate it would feel to put the teen on a trike like so?:

Young man! You have left your wallet on the couch again. The rule is that it must be put in the drawer. You are grounded.

When parents put teens on trikes, they not only deprive their children of the opportunity to practice making wise choices, they also foment a battle of the wills which alienates the child. They not only have lost control over the child, but have also lost the opportunity to provide much needed guidance. Teens are biologically programmed to seek autonomy. They aren't biologically programmed to fight with you! A one year old would fight with you too if you prevented him from learning to walk. If you support your teen in his efforts to become autonomous, there is no reason you can't retain your close, loving and respectful relationship with him.

To summarize, we want to start with strong structure and control when our children are young, and gradually move towards giving them more and more control of their own lives.

This is what I believe Dorothy Canfield Fisher meant in the quote at the beginning of this chapter, when she said that our job is to "make leaning unnecessary."

For today's exercise, list some ways you might be putting your child on an inappropriate bicycle, and list how you could do it more appropriately.

_____

_____

_____

_____

_____

_____

_____

_____

_____

_____

_____

_____

_____

_____

Next we will move on to studying the development of the psyche. This will help you to understand why it is unhealthy both to give young children too much choice, and to give teens too little.

Exercise Six

THE PSYCHE

Before bringing together the concepts of the four skills and the three bicycles we need to add one more idea. This exercise is a heady one but please bear with me because this stuff is really important. And don't worry, it will soon make sense.

When scientists of any kind try to understand a phenomenon, the first thing they do is cut it up, and categorize the pieces. Psychologists, since Freud, have categorized the contents of our mind (thoughts and feelings) into three groups - the id, the ego and the superego. For convenience we will call them the Inner Child, Adult, and Parent, respectively, as was done by psychologist Eric Berne.

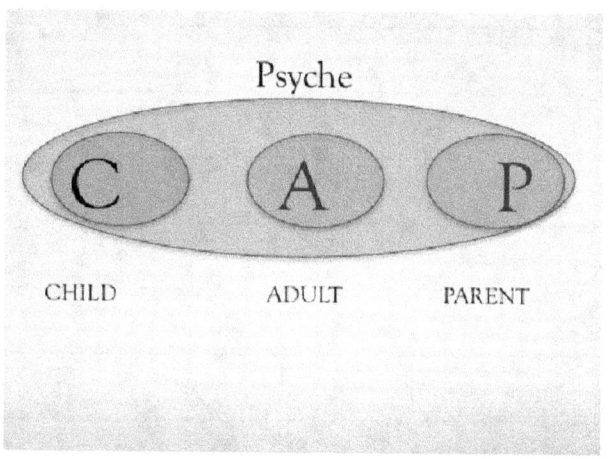

Figure B

The group of thoughts/feelings that is categorized as the INNER CHILD includes those that have to do with the expansion of the individual self in relation to the world. They are those instincts and drives that serve to protect the individual and to bring him pleasure and procreation. They usually originate as feelings, and are primarily concerned with the present - "I want it right now." "I want cookies. I want more power, more stuff, more room, more rights. I want sex. I want pleasure."

The group of thoughts/feelings that is categorized as the INNER PARENT includes those that have to do with containing the individual self in relation to the world. They usually originate as thoughts, and are concerned with what is right and wrong; what one should and shouldn't do. These concepts are learned from the adults who take care of us as we are growing up - parents, teachers, religious leaders, etc. They keep us from bothering or hurting other people, and often relate to our future well-being. "I shouldn't eat so many cookies. I might feel sick later. It's wrong to have more power, stuff, rights, than other people. I must be courteous and patient."

The group of thoughts/feelings that is categorized as the INNER ADULT are logical, based on our relationship with the real world. It is the ego that gives us our sense of being a separate "Self." It is from this base that we can move on to spiritual experience.

For today's exercise list something your inner child might say to you:

_____

_____

_____

_____

_____

List something your inner parent says to you:

_____

_____

_____

_____

_____

How does your inner adult respond?

_____

_____

_____

_____

_____

When the Inner Child is too dominant, a person lacks impulse control, and acts irrationally, with little regard for the needs of others or for his own future. On the other hand, when the Inner Parent is too dominant, she lives like a robot, without passion or zest for life, fearfully and mechanically following rules. In a healthy psyche, the Inner Adult is in control, hearing and considering both the desires of the Inner Child, and the admonitions of the Inner Parent, and then making rational decisions about the best overall course of action. If you consider passion to be the Inner Child, reason to be the Inner Parent, and the seafaring soul to be the Inner Adult, then the following poem describes the necessary balance between all three:

Your reason and your passion are the rudder and the sails
of your seafaring soul.
If either your sails or your rudder be broken,
you can but toss and drift, or else be held at a standstill in mid-seas.
For reason, ruling alone, is a force confining;
and passion, unattended, is a flame that burns to its own destruction.
Therefore, let your soul exalt your reason to the height of passion,
that it may sing;
And let it direct your passion with reason,
that your passion may live through its own daily resurrection,
and like the phoenix, rise above its own ashes.
—Kahlil Gibran, The Prophet

At birth a child is all Inner Child. He is said to be "undifferentiated," meaning that he doesn't have a sense that he is a separate being. Everything is one big experience to him. He certainly has no Inner Parent. If he feels like sticking his finger up your nose, he will stick his finger up your nose. He won't have a thought inside that says "I feel like sticking my finger up this grownup's nose, but I'd better not; I'd better stop myself from doing that, because that would be impolite." See Figure C.

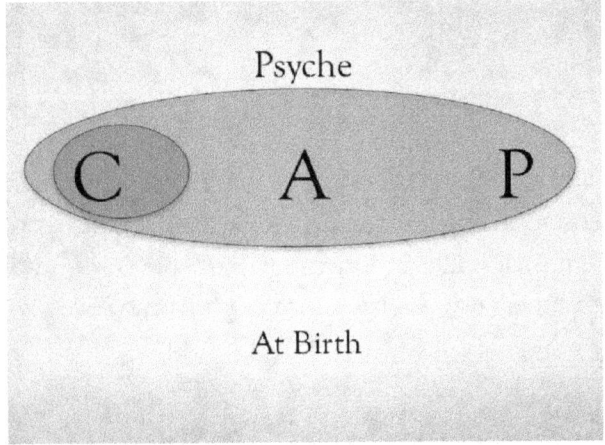

Figure C

Gradually, small 'islands' of Inner Adult develop as the child becomes more aware of his own existence. You can notice this through his language: At age 2 he says, "want ball," but towards age 3 it becomes "Aden want ball" and then eventually, "I want ball." According to psychologist, Carl Jung, the Inner Adult is created out of the pressure between the wants of the Inner Child and the restraints against it. He says, "There is no birth of consciousness without pain." Since the child has no Inner Parent to place restraint against his Inner Child, this restraint is provided by his environment - namely you. "Sorry son, can't do that." See Figure D.

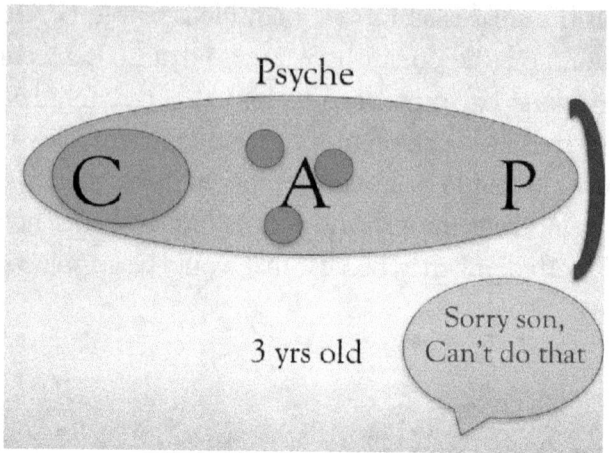

By the time the child is 5 or 6, her Inner Adult is congealed and she has a sense of being a separate being. She has constructed an inner pseudo-parent, that is like an inner replica of you. It sounds like "I want to steal my brother's toy, but my mom won't let me." See Figure E.

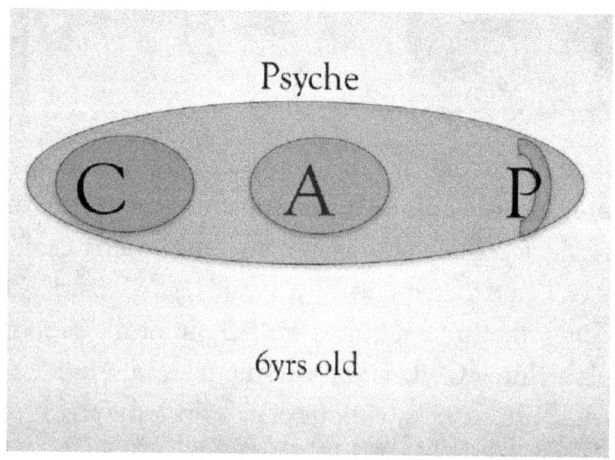

Figure E

At about age 9, the child has a fully developed psyche, with Inner Child, Adult, and Parent. See Figure F. He can make decisions in

34

a mature way, with the Inner Adult hearing both the wants of the Inner Child and the constraints of the Inner Parent, before making decisions. But this is like first learning to ride a bike-the child needs training wheels because he is just beginning to try out this new decision making tool and still needs your support.

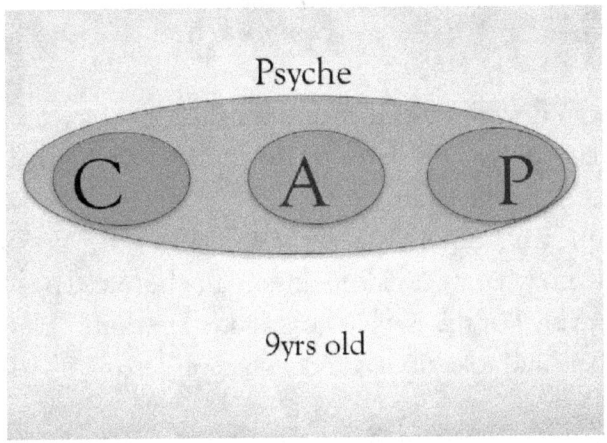

Gradually, around puberty, you can remove the training wheels and let the child make her own decisions with her own Inner Parent as the restraining force instead of you providing the restraining force. The young child, as you can now see, has no inner restraining force, and thus requires you to provide this by making the necessary life decisions for him. Your "no" can be a gift.

Exercise Seven

INNER FREEDOM

Most people do not really want freedom, because freedom involves responsibility, and most people are frightened of responsibility.
—*Sigmund Freud*

We can now put together the four skills, the bicycle analogy, and your understanding of the development of the psyche. What we hope to gain is called Inner Freedom.

In America, freedom is valued very highly. Why? Because we want to be able to do what we decide to do, and not be forced by someone else to do otherwise. But this is what I call Outer Freedom. "Hey man, I can hang out here and toke up, I can do whatever I want, it's a free country ain't it?"

Inner Freedom is an entirely different matter. It is the ability to manifest intentions that originate from the highest part of your Self. Though in America most of us have a great deal of Outer freedom, few of us have very much Inner Freedom.

The subject of Inner Freedom seems to be a crossroad of philosophy (Do we have free will, or is everything predestined?), psychology (What motivates man to make the decisions he makes?), and religion (What is sin? How do we follow God's will?). I like to work with the idea of Inner Freedom put forth by philosopher Rudolf Steiner, "An action is felt to be free to the extent that its reason stems from the ideal part of my individual being. Every other part of an action, regardless of whether this part is performed under the compulsion of nature or the constraint of a moral norm, is felt to be unfree."

And to paraphrase Steiner in modern psychological terms, an action is done with free will when it is decided from the Inner Adult (or in Steiner's terms 'the ideal part of my individual being'), with input from, but not compelled by, the Inner Child (or Steiner's 'compulsion of nature'), and with input from, but not constrained by, the Inner Parent (or Steiner's 'moral norm')

In reality it is rare that we actually practice Inner Freedom. Instead we are generally either compelled to act by our Inner Child, or constrained by our Inner Parent.

Exercise Eight

DECIDING VS. CHOOSING

Using the model of the Inner Adult, Parent, and Child, and letting the understanding you have of Inner Freedom be the definition for the word "deciding," see if you can distinguish the difference between deciding on one hand, and choosing on the other.

Don't peek ahead. Really think about it!

Deciding means to:

_____

_____

_____

Choosing means to:

_____

_____

_____

"My subjects (self actualized people) make up their own minds, come to their own decisions, are self-starters, and are responsible for themselves and their own destinies. It is a subtle quality, difficult to describe in words, and yet profoundly important.

"They taught me to see as profoundly sick, abnormal, or weak what I had always taken for granted as humanly normal; namely, that too many people do not make up their own minds, but have their minds made up for them by salesmen, advertisers, parents, propagandists, TV, newspapers, and so on. They are pawns to be moved by others rather than self-moving, self-determining individuals. Therefore they are apt to feel helpless, weak, and totally determined."

Abraham Maslow, Motivation and Personality

DECIDING VS CHOOSING ANSWER

Deciding is the process of the Inner Adult considering both the wants of the Inner Child, as well as the constraints of the Inner Parent, and then making a decision as to the best overall course of action.

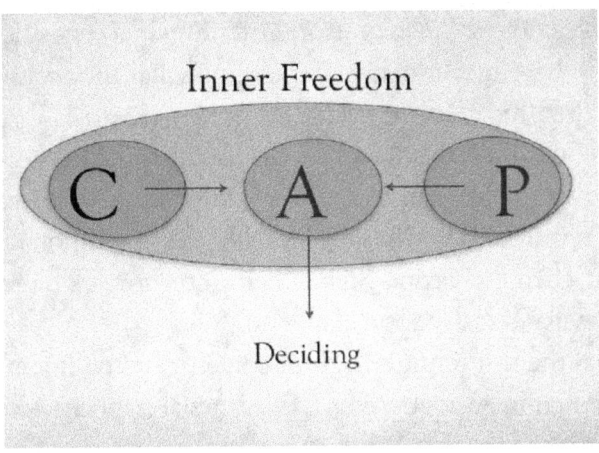

Choosing is simply acting according to the inclinations of the Inner Child. "I want chocolate."

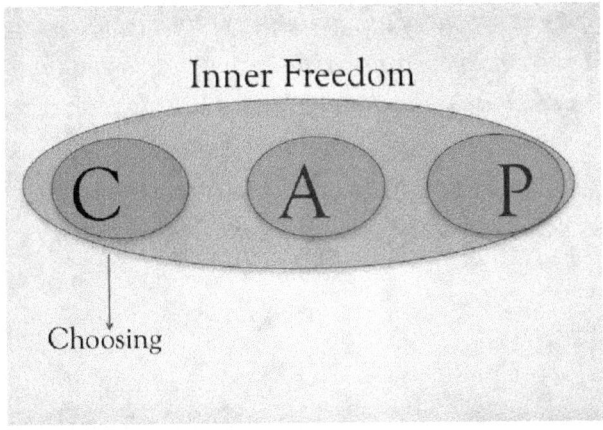

Please note that until a child has an internalized Inner Parent, it is *not possible* for him to truly decide. He can only make a choice. And that is an entirely different animal!

Often pop psychologists advise new parents to be sure to give their young children choices in order to help develop their ability to make decisions. But this advice makes no sense when you realize that at this young age it isn't even possible to develop the ability to make decisions - only to make choices. Unless you are parenting in a very strict way, your children will have no difficulty announcing what they want! By giving young children too many choices, we don't strengthen their ability to make decisions, but instead, reinforce their compulsion to do whatever their Inner Child tells them to do. While this is the first of the important 4 skills, if they always do what they feel like doing, without any practice *not* doing it, then the second skill, of being able to *not* do what they feel like doing, will never develop.

This is the first of the two most common parenting mistakes that I see happening in America today. This is what happens when toddlers are put on twelve-speeds.

The fact that the conventions always flourish in one form or another only proves that the vast majority of mankind do not choose their own way, but convention, and consequently develop not themselves, but a method and a collective mode of life, at the cost of their own wholeness.
The mechanism of convention keeps people unconscious for in that state they can follow their accustomed tracks like blind brutes, without the need for conscious decision.
Personality (i.e. self actualization) can never develop unless the individual chooses his own way, consciously and with moral deliberation.
Carl Jung

Exercise Eight B

INNER FREEDOM EXERCISE

Think of a situation in which you felt unfree.

_____

_____

_____

_____

_____

A situation where you felt unfree because you were compelled by your Inner Child would look something like this: "I decided to work on my thesis every day for 2 hours, but I didn't today because I didn't feel like it." "I want to lose weight but I felt like eating that whole pizza, and I did!" "I know I should have called to cancel that appointment instead of just not showing up, but I just couldn't bring myself to make the call." "I know I shouldn't yell at her, but I just couldn't help myself."

A situation where you felt unfree because you were constrained by your Inner Parent would look something like "He seemed nice but you aren't supposed to go out with younger men." "I was so mad at what she had done, but I didn't say anything because it's frowned upon in my office to complain." "I've always dreamed of opening a restaurant, but I'm getting an engineering degree so I can make a good living."

Remember the 4 skills we want to impart to our children? The ability to do what you want and to _not_ do what you want. The ability to give over to others and to _not_ give over to others? Put all together they equal Inner Freedom

* The first skill of honoring our wants is getting input from our Inner Child.

* The second skill of _not_ honoring our wants is not being compelled

by the Inner Child.

 * The third skill of giving over to others is hearing the input from the Inner Parent.

 * The fourth skill of *not* giving over to others, is to not be constrained by the Inner Parent.

 Now that we understand the workings of the psyche, we can use this knowledge to better understand how to help our children learn those four skills so they can grow up to attain Inner Freedom.

Exercise Nine

THE BOOT CAMP - MAYHEM CONTINUUM

OK, so we understand what Inner Freedom is, and we've established that for our children to attain our goals for them they must develop Inner Freedom. And we also understand that for our children to attain Inner Freedom, they need to develop the four skills. But how does the way we parent affect the development of the four skills in our children?

It's hard to look at our parenting methods scientifically, since there are as many methods as there are parents. But we are starting with the premise that the way most of us parent now, unconsciously compelled by the habits and impulses that we most likely learned from our own parents, is fundamentally flawed. And, as in any science, in order to move out of this realm of unconscious parenting and into a place where we have the ability to make conscious parenting choices, we must learn to draw lines, dissect our methods, categorize our actions, even just theoretically, in order to give us back the conscious awareness of what we are doing, so that we can parent by choice, rather than habit. To this end, I use a simple continuum of parenting methods that I call the Boot Camp-Mayhem Continuum.

```
   Needs              CONSCIOUS              Too
    not               PARENTING             much
    met                   |                choice
                          |
                          |
BOOT CAMP_____MAYHEM
   authoritarian   |   authoritative   |   permissive
```

On the Boot Camp end of this continuum, parents control the child by force, punishment, blame, and shame. The child is expected to "behave," which means conforming to the needs of the parents. On the Mayhem end, parents focus on filling the child's desires, and try to avoid saying no, for fear of making the child unhappy.

On the Boot Camp end of this continuum, we make decisions without regard to the needs of the child (much less his wants!). If you hear a child make a request of his parent, and hear the parent reply "No. I don't want you to," then this parent is probably practicing Boot Camp parenting. If the parent answered "No, because later it will hurt you" or "No, because that would drive your Grandmother nuts right now" or even "No. I know it would be fun for you, but right now I have a big headache" then this parent is practicing conscious parenting. Just because a parent says "no" doesn't mean he is Boot Camp parenting. What makes it Boot Camp parenting is that the decision is made based solely on the whims of the parent, without considering the wants of the child.

On the Mayhem end of the continuum, the inclinations of the child rule the home, without regard to the needs of other people, or the long-term benefit of the child. Here, decisions are made because of what a child "feels like" doing, rather than from a place of wisdom deciding what is best. "Carla needs a cookie right now dear. Can you pull off the highway and try to find a store?" Both extremes are unhealthy.

Whenever I work with a continuum, I find it helpful to examine the positives and negatives of each of the two extremes. As an exercise, see if you can identify what might be positive about each extreme.

Also identify what might be negative. How would it be for the parents? How would it affect the child?

POSITIVES   NEGATIVES

MAYHEM

_____   _____
_____   _____
_____   _____
_____   _____
_____   _____
_____   _____

BOOT CAMP

_____   _____
_____   _____
_____   _____
_____   _____
_____   _____

The following exercises list some positives and negatives that parents in my workshops have come up with. Compare their list with yours.

Jane Martin

Exercise Ten

THE BOOT CAMP - MAYHEM CONTINUUM

The Dangers of the Boot Camp Method

1. THE CHILD'S NEEDS ARE UNMET

The primary weakness of the Boot Camp Method is that it very often doesn't meet the needs of the child.

While it is my observation that our society is currently leaning heavily towards the Mayhem end, with the result being a disordered and scattered family life, I have also seen families suddenly go all the way to the Boot Camp end, possibly as a reaction to the difficulties inherent in the Mayhem lifestyle. One blatant example is the practice of "Ferberizing" a baby - which was embraced nationally with amazing speed in the late 1980's. On the advice of Dr. Ferber, director of the Center for Pediatric Sleep Disorders at Children's Hospital Boston, parents would steel themselves against the cries of their baby, and allow him to cry himself to sleep. Theoretically, this taught the baby to "put himself to sleep," thereby lessening the load for parents. But I feel that what it really taught the baby was that it was futile to cry; no one was going to respond to his needs anyway. This was so clearly neglectful of a basic human biological need, that psychologists finally started speaking out and eventually Dr. Ferber recanted his advice. But much harm had already been done.

Human beings have many biological expectations. When we're born we expect to be cared for in certain ways that have been common to our species for thousands of years. When these expectations are not met, it causes psychological, and in some cases, physical damage. Sometimes our children's needs are inconvenient. Feeding on demand, driving her to a important party even though you're tired, taking care of them during the night when you're sleepy; all these things aren't what you might "feel like" doing at the time. But sometimes, Conscious Parenting requires us to practice Skill #2, doing something we don't feel like doing. Boot

Camp parenting ignores this skill and puts the parents' desires ahead of the needs of the child.

2. SKILL #4 (Not doing what other people say to do) IS NOT LEARNED

The Boot Camp Method teaches obedience, not morality. The child doesn't learn Skill #4, having the ability to sometimes NOT do what other people say.

This is often called authoritarian parenting. It teaches children to obey, not to make good decisions themselves. In 1961, Stanley Milgram, a professor of psychology at Yale University, performed an experiment, which demonstrated the detrimental effects of this type of parenting. In a controlled psychological experiment, 65% of normal Americans were willing to give an apparently harmful electric shock (up to 450 volts) simply because an authority figure told them to. They knew the victim hadn't done anything to deserve being shocked, and they received no reward, nor escaped any consequences themselves for doing so. They were simply unable to think for themselves, to decide on their own what was right and what was wrong. They were trained to obey authority and they did. Not coincidentally, this was the dominant form of parenting in Nazi Germany.

3. SKILL #1 (Doing what he wants) IS NOT LEARNED

Boot Camp parenting tends to breed either angry or repressed children. The child doesn't learn Skill #1, doing what he wants.

The "force" of authoritarian parenting represses the Inner Child and the child loses touch with what she wants or needs; loses her passion for life. Among other things this interferes with the development of a healthy Inner Adult. The Boot Camp parent makes decisions based on her own wants and needs without taking into consideration the needs of her child. The child is forced again and again to forego her own desires. There isn't enough psychological space for the child. The natural instincts toward pleasure, growth, and expression are obstructed so often that the expansive force of the Inner Child must find another outlet. Sometimes the energy funnels into anger directed outwards through violence, stealing, lying, vandalism, bullying etc. Sometimes this anger energy is directed back upon oneself, and is expressed through low self-esteem, chronic illness, cutting, eating disorders, or depression.

If the child is angry, when he becomes a teenager and can no longer be controlled by force, the parents will have a very difficult time controlling his behavior. Even worse, if the child reacts to Boot Camp parenting by repressing her personality, the result can be a child with low self-esteem who feels herself to be unworthy, insignificant, or just plain bad.

The Dangers of the Mayhem Method

1. THE CHILD BECOMES BRATTY

In the Mayhem Method the distinction between wants and needs is lost and the result is what we call "brattiness." Infants' wants are the same as their needs, but once they become toddlers, children will have many wants that aren't really needs at all.

When parents fall all over themselves trying to satisfy every whim of their beloved child, the child quite naturally begins to believe that it is absolutely necessary that his every whim be fulfilled. There is no distinction between needs and wants, so in circumstances when it isn't possible to fill his *wants*, the child becomes frantic, as if some vital *need* is not being met. This fear compels him to use all his power to get that want filled, since to him it seems like a need! The next time you witness a child acting like a "brat," look deeper and see if you sense a fear there. Often if you just tell the child: "It's OK if you don't get what you want right now. You will be fine," he will calm down immediately. (Didn't The Rolling Stones teach us this? "You can't always get what you want. But if you try sometimes, you just might find, you get what you need...") Such frantic behavior can be quite stressful for families facing a full blown war every time a child doesn't get what he wants.

2. SKILL #2 (Being able to do something he doesn't "feel like" doing - and the ability to refrain from doing something he feels like doing.) IS NOT LEARNED

To live in society with other people, each of us needs to find that balance between self and other. By occasionally practicing the art of relinquishing his desires in favor of those of others, a child learns that this is part of life, and that he *can* do it, and still be fine. He also learns to delay gratification in the interest of his long-term benefit. As a teen, when faced with the decision to do his homework or to hang out with friends, the child who has spent his life deciding on the basis of what he "feels like doing," will have a difficult time choosing to do his homework. Then, all of a sudden, the parents try to jump back over to the Boot Camp method, by imposing harsh punishments on the teenager in an attempt to rectify the damage done. This is unfortunate because this is just the time when a child is biologically programmed to detach from his parents and become independent. The time to teach the art of doing what you don't feel like is in the early years.

If you think back to the exercise about the psyche (inner child, adult, and parent), you will remember that Inner Freedom was defined as the ability to decide with input from, but not compelled by the Inner Child and input from, but not constrained by the Inner Parent. This kind of decision is made from the Inner Adult and the ability to do this is the foundation for further spiritual growth. Here "deciding" is distinguished from "choosing" - choosing being to simply state the inclination of the Inner Child. This choosing isn't Inner Freedom, because you are being compelled by the Inner Child. Part of Inner Freedom is having the option, the ability, to *not* do what the id says if you decide not to. "I want to eat 10 ice cream cones," says the Inner Child. "Ice cream cones are bad," says the Inner Parent. "I'll have just one ice cream cone," decides the ego. An unfree person will eat 10 if he is compelled by the Inner Child or none if constrained by the ideas of the Inner Parent.

Remember a young child is still just a big Inner Child. He doesn't yet have the psychological capacity to make decisions, only to make choices. Parents wanting to be sure their children grow up to be decisive adults, want to give them early practice at decision making. But all they are doing is just giving them practice stating the inclinations of the Inner Child. The only way they will be able to act contrary to those inclinations is if the adult provides limits. So this skill, to *not* do what the Inner Child says, is one that is not developed with the Mayhem method of parenting, and thus these children grow up unable to do other than what they "feel like." According to child psychologist, Jean Piaget, a young child lacks the cognitive ability to make the future real. This inability leads to the epidemic of obesity, addiction, debt, unfulfilled goals, and directionless lives that we see. This is what Eugene Schwartz meant when he said:

> *"The power to decide, I would claim, is built upon the ability to accept the decisions of adults in one's youth."*
> —Eugene Schwartz,
> *Authority and Discipline in the Life of the Child*

In other words, by learning to accept an adult's decisions that are contrary to his own desires, a child learns that it is OK to not do what his Inner Child says. Then later if his Inner Adult decides to do something other than what the Inner Child says, he will be able to accept it. He will be free.

3. UNWISE DECISIONS ARE MADE

The negative consequences of unwise decisions can't be avoided, and in Mayhem Method households, with the child directing the family life, many unwise decisions are made.

I once overheard the mother of a toddler say "But he wouldn't go to bed until 12:30 and now we are all so tired. He just ruined our day!" Obviously, when that child didn't "want" to go to bed, he was not considering the negative consequences for the next day. He was too young to be expected to understand the consequences of his choice. That is the responsibility of the parent. We think we are giving our children what they want, but eventually the consequences hurt both them and us.

4. THE CHILD FEELS UNSAFE

The next problem with the Mayhem approach is that when a child senses that she is in charge, that she's running the show, she feels unsafe, and rightly so, since she is certainly not equipped with the knowledge necessary to make wise decisions about her life. The usual reaction children have is to act out more and more until the parent takes back control, thus relieving the child's anxiety.

5. SKILL #3 (Giving over to others) IS NOT LEARNED

Today's teachers are being confronted by a problem that seems to be growing every year - keeping order in the classroom. The problem is labeled many things; "Kids don't listen," "Kids have no impulse control," "Kids are inconsiderate of each other," "Kids lack common courtesy," "Kids talk out in class, are impolite and impudent." And most commonly this problem is described as "Kids lack respect."

According to the Encarta Dictionary, respect means, "To show consideration or thoughtfulness in relation to somebody or something." A young child, being just a big Inner Child with not too much Inner Parent in his psyche, wouldn't get a natural inner impulse stimulating him to consider someone else's needs. This is the kind of impulse that comes from the Inner Parent, not the Inner Child. This is a skill, and hopefully a habit, that must be taught by the parents. When parenting decisions focus only on the wants of the child, without including in the process the wants of other people, the child doesn't develop this habit of considering other people. This skill needs to be modeled by the parents. "Yes Megan, I see that you want to use the hose up here on the porch, but consider also that Grandma would be uncomfortable if you got her dress wet." Now Megan practices the habit of considering Grandma. When she goes to school, she will be in the habit of considering the needs of the other children. Since most American parents practice Mayhem parenting, it is not surprising that an inability to show respect is becoming endemic in the schools.

The Positive Aspects of the Extremes

So those were some negative aspects to the far reaches of the Boot Camp - Mayhem Continuum. What about positive aspects? Here are some that parents in my workshops came up with:

Boot Camp - Life is the way you, as parents, want it. Your children don't bother you or get in your way.

Mayhem - you enjoy giving to your child, and vicariously feel their happiness. (Short term though it is!)

Both - You don't have to be awake. You don't have to be conscious. You get to avoid the difficult task of decision-making. On the Boot Camp end, you do what you want. On the Mayhem end, you do what the child wants. It's a clear and simple formula.

Exercise Eleven

THE BALANCE POINT – CONSCIOUS PARENTING

On the Mayhem end of the continuum, decisions are made based on what the child feels like doing; on the Boot Camp end, on the whims of the parent. At each extreme, parenting is a simple formula. But staying in the middle requires consciousness. It is difficult to make conscious decisions. Yet isn't that our job? Otherwise, we could hire robots to raise our children.

The Two Generals

Consider that you have the opportunity to choose a person to be President. There are two contenders, both of whom were generals in the army. When faced with a decision as to whether to have the army launch an attack, the first general made a quick decision, and went home. But the second general stayed up all night, considering all the options, the suffering the attack might cause, as well as the consequences of deciding not to attack. He took his responsibility very seriously. Which person would you expect to be a better President?

_____

In the same way, to be a better parent, to make conscious decisions rather than automatically following someone's whims, requires a lot more mental effort.

Now we are ready to talk about how to make this effort.

The Point of Balance

We've discussed the pitfalls of the extremes. Now how do we find the optimal midpoint? Where is the point of balance?

If you break the Boot Camp - Mayhem Continuum up into three

sections, or, in other words, divide a child's desires up into three categories, we can label them as follows:

BOOT CAMP_____MAYHEM
     Needs | OK Wants | Not OK wants

Needs: When presented with a request from a child, first determine whether the request, or any part of it, is to satisfy a human need. If so, say yes, even if it is uncomfortable for you. For example, getting up and taking care of an upset during the night even though you are tired.

List some needs your child has expressed to you:

_____

Did you say yes to all of them?

_____

OK Wants: The second category encompasses your child's requests that if they're met won't hurt the child or bother anyone else, and don't harm the environment. You'd happily say yes to these. "Sure you can have an apple."

List some OK Wants of your child:

_____

Did you say yes to them?

_____

Not OK Wants: In the third category are desires of the child that are not needs, and which, if fulfilled, would hurt other people, the child himself, or the environment. To these, you would say a firm "No." "Sorry but if you eat all three of these ice cream cones you'll end up with a stomachache."

List some Not OK Wants of your child:

_____

Did you say no to them?

_____

BOOT CAMP_____MAYHEM
    Needs | OK Wants | Not OK wants

    Yes   Yes   No

In conclusion - For the optimal health of your child, I suggest granting the child's requests up to, but not beyond, the point where to do so would hurt other people, himself, or the environment.

Two questions remain. One is how to distinguish a want from a need. The other is how to go about the difficult process of saying "no." The next exercises will address these questions.

The aim, to give your child as much as he wants, up to but not past the point where his wants will hurt another person, himself, or his environment, finding the balance between self and other, which we strive for in all relationships - is clearly articulated in the following quote:

"It is the work of a true teacher to maintain a balance, during these stages, between an excessively strong expression of the youngster's own impulses against other people on the one hand, and the extinction of the personality, which results in a slavish subjugation to other people or to one's own desires, on the other."
—Bernard Lievegoed, Phases of Childhood

Exercise Twelve

MORE BOOT CAMP – MAYHEM EXERCISES

Read the following conversations and see if you can tell which parenting method - Boot Camp, Mayhem or Conscious Parenting – is being used. Circle the answer. Be sure to ask yourself if the child's request is a need, an OK want, or a Not OK want.

1. Six year old Katie asks, "May I have another serving of broccoli?"
   Parent "No, you've had enough."

   Boot Camp / Mayhem / Conscious

2. Four year old Brad is running around in a restaurant interrupting other patrons' dinners.
   His mother explains to the waitress that Brad is a very energetic and exuberant boy and he needs this kind of space in order to not feel constrained.

   Boot Camp / Mayhem / Conscious

3. Megan, 12 years old, asks her mom if she can join the rest of the girls in her class who are going to the mall.
   Her mother replies, "I'd rather you stayed here."

   Boot Camp / Mayhem / Conscious

4. Six year old Jessa asks her dad if she and her friends can do playdough.
   Her dad replies "Playdough sounds fun, but I have to finish this report before we leave in an hour and I won't have time to clean up the playdough."
   Jessa says, "How about if you set the alarm clock and tell us when to stop and we'll clean it up ourselves?"
   "OK! Deal!"

   Boot Camp / Mayhem / Conscious

ANSWERS

1. If Katie has a tendency to overeat, then this might be a Conscious Parenting decision. Or, if it were junk food that Katie was asking for then possibly the parent would be setting healthy limits for the child. But if she is asking for healthy food, meaning that she is expressing hunger, it would seem like Boot Camp parenting to invalidate her expression of hunger by stating that she "had enough."

2. If Brad was made to sit in a desk all day in school, then this exuberant movement might be considered a need. In this case, his mother could take him outside the restaurant to run around for a while. But otherwise it would benefit Brad to learn the skill of sitting quietly so that he can be in our society without provoking anger from other people. This mother is Mayhem Parenting.

3. It's Ok for the mom to have a preference and bring it into consideration when making this decision. However, it appears that the daughter's preference was given no weight in the decision. This is Boot Camp Parenting.

4. This Conscious Parenting decision took into account the needs and wants of both the parent and the child. It taught Jessa that what she wants is important (Skill #1) and that it's also important to consider the other person too (Skill #3). She even got to make good use of her creative problem solving skills.

Exercise Thirteen

RIDING BICYCLES ALONG THE BOOT CAMP – MAYHEM CONTINUUM

In putting together the ideas of the Boot Camp – Mayhem Continuum and the three kinds of bicycles, people sometimes think that I am advising them to Boot Camp parent their young children and then Mayhem parent their teens. Reasonable mistake!

I'd like to ask you to envision the ideas this way: I am advising you to aim for the middle of the Boot Camp – Mayhem continuum at all times. Because your young children have not yet developed their Inner Parent, which would allow them to consider other peoples' needs, they don't have the ability to stay in the middle of the continuum. So I am suggesting that you force them to be there. This is the tricycle, which gives no options for left and right leaning. As the child gains the ability to consider others, and to stay in the center of the Boot Camp – Mayhem Continuum on his own, I suggest using training wheels and letting him try it out a bit on his own (within limits). And then gradually you can let go of the bike and just watch and be sure your teen is staying in the center on her own.

Please don't confuse a Boot Camp parent with a Conscious Parent saying "no." A parent who is firm with his young child can be either a Conscious Parent saying no after making a decision considering the needs and wants of all people concerned, or he might be a Boot Camp parent saying "no" after only considering his own wants and needs, and neglecting to consider those of his child. As an outside observer it is sometimes hard to tell, but they are in no way the same thing.

On the other hand, please don't confuse a Mayhem parent saying "yes" with a Conscious Parent saying "yes." The parents of my 17 year old daughter's friends might think I am a Mayhem parent since I have no rules and no punishments for my daughter. It might seem to them that I "let her do anything" and therefore I am not parenting well. But they can also see that my daughter makes wise choices. She gets her homework done and done well without my involvement. She takes care of her responsibilities. And though I have no curfew for her, she tells her friends, "I'm going home now because otherwise I'll be tired tomorrow." What sense would there be in making rules for a child like this? On the rare occasion she appears to be making a mistake, I simply draw her attention to it. While I have let go of the bike, I am still watching that it is staying in the center of the continuum.

For today's exercise, think about the last time you said no to your child.

What did she want? _____

Was it a need? _____

Did you consider the need? _____

Were you boot camp parenting or conscious parenting?

_____

Think about the last time you said yes to your child.

What was his want/need? _____

What reasons might have compelled you to say no?

_____

Did you consider these reasons? _____

Were you mayhem or conscious parenting?

_____

Jane Martin

"But now we are being confronted by a new possibility of pathology of psychological affluence; that is, of suffering from the consequences (apparently) of being loved and cared for devotedly, of being adored, admired, applauded, and listened to self-effacedly, of being given the center of the stage, of having loyal servants, of having every here-and-now wish granted, even of being the objects of self-sacrifice and self-abnegation.

"It is true that we just don't know much about these new phenomena, certainly not in any developed scientific sense. All we have are strong suspicions, widespread clinical impressions, the slowly hardening opinion of child psychologists and educators that merely and only basic need gratification is not enough, but that some experience with firmness, toughness, frustration, discipline, and limits is also needed by the child. Or to say it another way, basic need gratification had better be defined more carefully because it so easily slips over into unbridled indulgence, self-abnegation, total permissiveness, overprotection, and toadyness. Love and respect for the child must at the very least by integrated with love and respect for oneself as a parent and for adulthood in general. Children are certainly persons, but they are not experienced persons. They must be counted on to be unwise about many things, and positively stupid about some."

—Abraham Maslow, Motivation and Personality

Exercise Fourteen

WANTS VS. NEEDS

As discussed earlier, when deciding when to say yes, and when to say no, the first consideration is whether the stated desire is a need or just a want.

What do human beings need? This is a huge question, one which philosophers and psychologists have been discussing and debating for years.

The simplest answer is that we need safety, food, water, warmth... and love. It has in fact been shown that without love, babies will die, even when they are provided with adequate physical needs.

But these are the needs we have just to stay alive. Obviously we want more for our children. We want them to be able to reach their full potential, which adds significantly, of course, to our list of needs.

For simplicity, let's say that a child needs:

1. To have his biological expectations met.

2. To provide the barrier, the fence, the limits, so that his natural desires don't go too far.

Put another way, he needs:

1. Unconditional love (support)

2. Conditional love (a push towards growth)

Consider your children.

Do they receive both unconditional and conditional love?

_____

Which caregivers tend to give which kind of love?

_____

Does this explain any of the seeming conflicts and differences of opinion between you and other caregivers?

_____

If your tendency is to give unconditional love, can you honor and respect the importance of the conditional love that another caregiver brings to your child?

_____

And if your tendency is to give conditional love, can you honor and respect the importance of the unconditional love that another caregiver brings to your child?

_____

Exercise Fifteen

AN INFANT'S NEEDS

With respect to infants' needs, I can't do better than to simply quote Jean Liedloff, author of the Continuum Concept. The continuum concept is the idea that in order to achieve optimal physical, mental and emotional development, human beings—especially babies—must be exposed to the kind of experiences our ancestors lived through during the long process of the evolution of our species. For an infant, these include such experiences as...

- "constant physical contact with his mother (or another familiar caregiver as needed) from birth;

- sleeping in his parents' bed, in constant physical contact, until he leaves of his own volition (often about two years);

- breastfeeding "on cue" — nursing in response to his own body's signals;

- being constantly carried in arms or otherwise in contact with someone, usually his mother, and allowed to observe (or nurse, or sleep) while the person carrying him goes about his or her business — until the infant begins creeping, then crawling on his own impulse, usually at six to eight months;

- having caregivers immediately respond to his signals (squirming, crying, etc.), without judgment, displeasure, or invalidation of his needs, yet showing no undue concern nor making him the constant center of attention;

- sensing (and fulfilling) his elders' expectations that he is innately social and cooperative and has strong self-preservation instincts, and that he is welcome and worthy.

In contrast, a baby subjected to modern Western childbirth and child-care practices often experiences...

- traumatic separation from his mother at birth due to medical intervention and placement in maternity wards, in physical isolation except for the sound of other crying newborns, with the majority of male babies further traumatized by medically unnecessary circumcision surgery;

- at home, sleeping alone and isolated, often after "crying himself to sleep";

- scheduled feeding, with his natural nursing impulses often ignored or "pacified";

- being excluded and separated from normal adult activities, relegated for hours on end to a nursery, crib or playpen where he is inadequately stimulated by toys and other inanimate objects;

- caregivers often ignoring, discouraging, belittling or even punishing him when he cries or otherwise signals his needs; or else responding with excessive concern and anxiety, making him the center of attention;

- sensing (and conforming to) his caregivers' expectations that he is incapable of self-preservation, is innately antisocial, and cannot learn correct behavior without strict controls, threats and a variety of manipulative "parenting techniques" that undermine his exquisitely evolved learning process.

Evolution has not prepared the human infant for this kind of experience. He cannot comprehend why his desperate cries for the fulfillment of his innate expectations go unanswered, and he develops a sense of wrongness and shame about himself and his desires. If, however, his continuum expectations are fulfilled — precisely at first, with more variation possible as he matures — he will exhibit a natural state of self-assuredness, well-being and joy. Infants whose continuum needs are fulfilled during the early, in-arms phase grow up to have greater self-esteem and become more independent than those whose cries go unanswered for fear of "spoiling" them or making them too dependent."

Excerpted from "Understanding The Continuum Concept," (continuum-concept.org/cc_defined.html). Reprinted with permission.

If you have a small child, for today's exercise, consider if there are any additions to your Stage 1 list that you'd like to make after considering Jean Liedloff's advice.

Exercise Sixteen

HUMAN NEEDS

Most of us have a sense of what an infant needs, because basically, their wants and their needs are the same. But once a child reaches the age of about three this is no longer the case. Then the question of wants vs. needs becomes more complicated. I find that often, in two parent families, around this age, the mother (or primary caregiver) is continuing to parent in the way she has been parenting - when the child wants something, she provides it. But soon the father, who has a more detached overview, begins to feel uncomfortable, and begins to encourage the mother to set more limits for the child. How wonderful that nature has provided both conditional and unconditional love!

The research on human needs is vast, but many psychologists feel comfortable with the simple list created by Abraham Maslow that he called the Hierarchy of Needs. Maslow's theory is that a human being will first be motivated to meet his basic, lower level needs, and once they are met, he will then turn his attention to his higher needs. You may notice in the diagram that the needs begin with the physical, then move to the emotional, the intellectual and finally the spiritual needs. While we may not need approval, or intellectual stimulation, or order, to stay alive, these things are necessary in order for us to achieve our highest potential.

So in distinguishing whether our child's request is a want or a need, we must keep this broader view of human needs in mind.

Maslow's Hierarchy of Needs:

Deficiency Level

1. Physiological - hunger, thirst, body comfort

2. Safety/Security - preventing danger

3. Belongingness/ Love - to be affiliated with others, to be accepted

4. Esteem - to achieve, to be competent, to gain approval and recognition

Growth Level

5. To know, to understand, to explore

6. Aesthetics - symmetry, order, beauty

Transcendent Level

7. Self Actualization - to realize one's potential

8. Transcendence

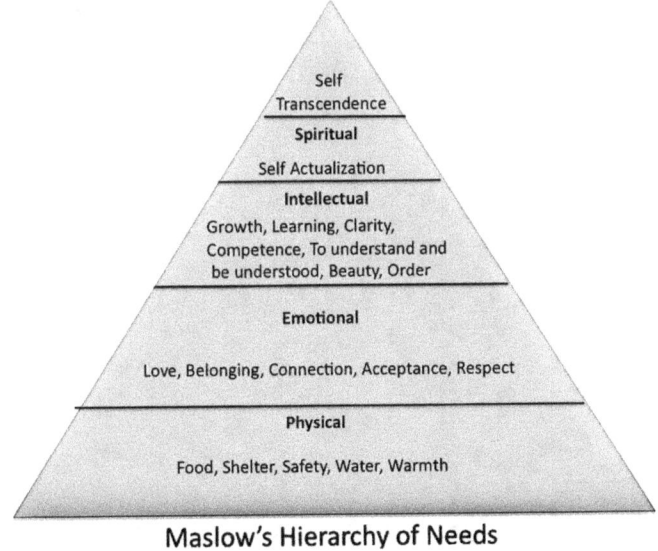

Maslow's Hierarchy of Needs

WANTS VS. NEEDS

Using Maslow's list of human needs, see if you can identify which need the following children are exhibiting by their behaviors.

1. Four year old Brian takes the water bottle from your friend's purse and begins to drink from it.

2. Eight year old Lila wants to join a dance class with her friends even though she has no interest in dancing.

3. A toddler reaches for Aunt Gertrude's $50,000 antique vase.

4. Tom spends 10 minutes every night cleaning up his room, packing his baseball cards to be ready for school the next day.

5. 14 year old Neil practices his basketball skills after school. He plans to try out for a team.

6. As I type this, my 21 year old son, Dave, is on a plane to India!

ANSWERS

1. Brian is trying to fill his physiological need for water. But the way he did it isn't acceptable.

2. Lila needs belongingness. If the class were too expensive for your budget you might have to say no, but you could be sure to arrange other situations for her to be with her friends.

3. This toddler is fulfilling his need to explore, but there is plenty for him to explore besides vases.

4. While some of us would love such a son, some might worry that he might be exhibiting overly neurotic behavior. But in any case he is fulfilling his need for order and aesthetics.

5. Neil is filling his need for esteem and competence.

6. Dave is working on his need for self-actualization and transcendence, and of course, exploring.

Exercise Seventeen

THE YIN AND YANG OF NEEDS

ALLOWING YANG

I would like to warn about a confusing phenomenon I notice in our society - especially among "new age" and religious people. I bring it up because it seems that this confusion may significantly harm our children. If you believe as I do that the psycho-spiritual development of human beings begins with the development of a healthy ego, a sense of being "someone" (psychological development), and then from this place of ego strength progressing to the next stage which is the spiritual growth towards transcendence of the ego - you can imagine this journey as first climbing a mountain (psychological growth through development of the ego) and then descending the mountain (spiritual growth towards transcendence of the ego). In the appendix there is a diagram of this process, which I call "The Coming Home Path," and is the essential theoretical linchpin of the End of the List Workshop of which this book is a part. Psychological growth, or climbing the mountain, requires upward moving or "yang" energies. These are energies that serve to expand the ego towards growth. Examples of yang energies would be taking control of your environment, using your anger to make sure your needs are considered and met, creating order from chaos, judging, classifying, and create dualities.

Descending the mountain, or spiritual growth, requires just the opposite, downward moving, "yin" energies, in which the individual self gives over to the environment. Examples are acceptance, forgiveness, integration of dualities, and allowing the environment to be as it is.

The very common and damaging mistake I see parents make with their children is that in an effort to teach their children the spiritual/religious values of humility, forgiveness, or acceptance, they try to enforce these downward moving energies on their child, before the child has reached the "top of the mountain." The result is that the downward movement represses the natural and healthy development of the ego, pushing the child down the left side of the mountain (repression) rather than serving his spiritual growth. I had a client whose minister father wouldn't allow him to use the word "I." The minister obviously wanted the child to be humble, to transcend the ego, but this just prevented the child from developing a healthy ego in the first place.

Another problem with enforcing yin energies too soon is that it often results in making our children feel shameful about attempting to fulfill their own needs. This puts them in a double bind - the deepest force of their being moves them to fill their own needs, but they are being told they are bad to make that effort. It will help avoid this problem if we can remember to look for the deepest motivation behind our child's behavior. Did he do it because he is "a little devil," "he's selfish," or "he's bad"? Or can we see the situation as a child trying to meet his own needs, to feel safe, to feel OK? And possibly the *way* he tried to meet those needs resulted in harm to others? If we can see with this new vision, then we can move from punishing him for being so-called "bad," to acknowledging him for trying to meet his needs, and showing him, teaching him, a better *way* to meet them. "Tony, I saw you hit Sally. I understand you felt very angry when she took your lunch. I would feel angry if someone took my lunch too. But by hitting her you have hurt her. What other ways could you have dealt with the situation that might have worked out better?" With an approach like this, instead of Tony having to deal with his lunch rights being violated, *and* with being told he is bad, *and* with the repercussions of the punishment, *and* with defending himself - he can, instead, freely and safely think in a more constructive way. He can do what we want him to do in the first place - learn a better way of behaving.

Jane Martin

ALLOWING YIN

At one workshop, a mother said that her 3 year old often threw fits if he couldn't complete a task in the way he had imagined it. For instance, he had intended to slice his sandwich himself, but she had unknowingly sliced it. The child insisted that she make a new sandwich so he could slice it.

The mother saw her son's impulse as his "biological imperative," a positive impulse to learn to become competent in the world (See Maslow's hierarchy above), so she judged her son's request to be a "need."

Another child gave her mother a tiny drawing. She thanked her daughter, but later discarded it. To the child this was a deep expression of her love, and when she found out that her mother had thrown it away, she was hurt. She then threw a fit, insisting that her mother retrieve it from the garbage man. The mother was distraught, believing that she was "unable to fill all my daughter's needs."

A child needs to eat, but not to eat every minute. He needs acceptance, but not all the time from every single person. She needs to explore and grow, but not every time the impulse is there.

And I'd like to point out that one could consider it a "need" for these children to be able to feel OK, even though they didn't get to cut the sandwich, or retrieve the drawing. They need the ability to feel OK letting things go, which is yin energy. These mothers were feeling so distraught about not being able to cater to their child's immediate impulses that they ended up conveying that sense of unease to their children.

Boot Camp parenting would lead a parent to say, "I don't care that you wanted to cut the sandwich. It's easier for me to do it myself. I'm not concerned with your growth and development."

A Mayhem Parent would say, "You aren't OK unless every whim, every impulse is fulfilled."

But Conscious Parenting would look at this situation, acknowledge the overall importance of the need for growth, but note that the child had plenty of experiences of challenge and growth during her day. It would be clear that the child didn't "need" to cut that sandwich, and would be just fine not doing it. The parent would then deeply feel the OK'ness, the safety of the situation, and convey that to the child. "I see that you wanted to cut the sandwich yourself. I'm sorry I cut it; I didn't know you wanted to. I wish I were magic and could uncut the sandwich!! But you will be just fine waiting until lunch tomorrow to cut a sandwich." The silliness, the smile, the kindness, and mainly the sense of calm from this parent, is much more valuable to the child than the growth experience of cutting a sandwich.

For today's exercise, consider these concepts in relation to your parenting in the past few days.

_____

_____

_____

_____

_____

_____

_____

_____

_____

_____

_____

Jane Martin

Exercise Eighteen

PUNISHMENT VS. CONSEQUENCES

Be careful of rules for your children
Rules diminish responsibility.
Be careful of rewards for your children.
Rewards diminish self-esteem.
Be careful of punishments for your children.
Punishments diminish trust.

Let lessons be imposed by the nature of things,
not by your own agendas,
or your own needs.
Integrity will replace rules.
Contentment will replace striving.
Spirituality will replace religion.
Songs will replace arguments.
Dances will replace battles.
—William Martin, The Parent's Tao Te Ching

Before discussing HOW to say no, I feel that it is imperative to consciously examine our own, possibly unconscious, attitudes regarding punishment. To do so we need to digress so that we can become clear about the difference between punishment and consequences.

Fill in your definition of punishment:

_____

_____

_____

_____

Fill in your definition of consequences:

_____

_____

_____

_____

I define punishment as the infliction of discomfort on the child, in the belief that he needs to suffer in order to be motivated to improve.

I define consequences as what might naturally occur, or what might logically occur as a result of undesirable behavior.

If a child writes on a wall, the consequence might be that she must scrub that wall clean, while punishment might be that she stays in for detention. Scrubbing puts the situation back to its rightful place, teaching the child to make amends; detention has no useful function other than to make her uncomfortable. The rationale is that the suffering will deter future transgressions. As you will see, this not only doesn't work very well, it also has a significant negative impact on the child.

There are many "habits" of society - beliefs, norms, accepted attitudes - that upon conscious examination, are found to serve no one. I ask you to examine the notion of punishment carefully and then to decide for yourself whether you choose to accept this societal norm in your life, or whether you would rather rely on alternative methods, which are based on a more positive view of basic human nature.

Many generations ago, when Puritan attitudes governed American society even more than they do today, children were thought of as intrinsically evil and it was seen as the job of the parent to beat this evil out of the child. The aim was to break the will of the child, and the supposed result was a "good" child, one who was seen but not heard, obedient, submissive, passive. Unfortunately, in the process, the child was disempowered, suppressed, and violated.

Only in the last century when we began to realize that violated children grew up to be violent parents, did schools begin to prohibit corporal punishment, and the government start to legislate human rights for children.

But while we have changed our methods, I wonder if we have changed our basic premise - namely, that a child is essentially evil. Because in my view, punishment of any kind has this as its sad premise.

If as you gaze at your infant's beautiful, pure and innocent face, you still hold this view, then you need read no further. But if you are having a difficult time perceiving your baby as inherently evil, then possibly you will come to share my belief in the essential goodness of every child.

With goodness rather than evil as our basic axiom, we are unlikely to find punishment to be a logical method of discipline.

We will no longer look at discipline as a way to beat the evil out of our children, but rather, as a way to teach our children to live in the world in a way that will be most beneficial to them and others.

What we want our child to learn is that if in an attempt to fulfill his own immediate desires, he acts in a way that adversely affects another person, or the environment, or his own future well being, he will eventually suffer the negative consequences of his actions. That is a basic natural law of the universe.

If he fulfills his desire to eat too much now, he will suffer indigestion later. If he takes more than his fair share, another person will become angry with him. If he destroys something in his environment, it will no longer be beautiful or functional for him.

So most of the time, it is in a person's own best interest to fulfill his desires only up to the point before he hurts his environment, another person, or his future self. Please note though, that it *is* in the best interests of a person to fulfill his desires! This is very important. We don't want to mistakenly teach our children that there is anything intrinsically wrong with fulfilling their desires. What we are discussing is that there are times when it is not in their best interests to fulfill those desires right then and there. It is the application of this concept that we hope to teach by discipline.

So the question becomes, which approach, punishment or consequences, better serves the goal of guiding the child to behaviors that will benefit both her and society?

Let's look at punishment. Think back to your own experience as a child. An adult, a person with absolute power over you, strikes you, humiliates you, or sends you to your room. How did you respond? With love, respect, or gratitude toward this person for teaching you? Did this motivate you to sit and think about how you could improve your personality and behavior? Or did you respond by feeling anger and hate, thinking thoughts of revenge, or at least feeling misunderstood. More likely the latter, and this kind of negative environment is not conducive to positive growth. This is why, I believe, punishment doesn't work.

Punishment teaches a child that:

You don't believe in her innate desire to do well and be good.
You believe she deserves to suffer. (She is likely to carry this belief
    into adulthood and feed it by causing her own suffering.)
You believe she is intrinsically bad.
You believe she has little worth.
That making a mistake isn't OK - and that after making a
    mistake it is necessary to suffer.
That guilt is a necessary consequence of making a mistake.
That doing "wrong" things is OK as long as you aren't caught.
That you are her enemy.

Consequences, on the other hand, teach a child that:

You believe in her desire to learn.
You trust that she will eventually learn to make wise choices for
    herself.
You expect her to take responsibility for her choices.
You would rather she NOT suffer (that is the ultimate goal of
    discipline, after all, that she have a good life, right?) and that is

exactly why you are making sure that she learns the natural laws of her world.

You are not her enemy, but her supporter and teacher.

Taking risks to grow and learn is OK, making mistakes in that process is inevitable and certainly we all make mistakes. It does not mean she is bad or worthless, and making a mistake isn't something to be feared.

If a mistake is made, the thing to do is not to feel guilty, but rather to rectify the mistake. A child learns to make amends, how to do it, and to learn from the mistake.

Here are some practical examples of the differences between the punishments and consequences:

A child makes a mess.

Punishment might be to show anger, remove TV privileges, or call the child a slob.

Consequence might be to show disappointment and to hand the child a sponge, supervising the cleanup but not doing it. "I still see watermelon under the table." This teaches the child to make amends, and gives him the skills to do it.

A child is screaming.

Punishment might be to say, "You are driving everyone crazy. Go to your room!"

Consequence might be to say, "Your loud screaming is hurting our ears. You may stay here quietly or go up to your room with the door closed and scream."

A child is late getting ready for school.

Punishment might be to say, "If you aren't ready on time, no play date tomorrow."

Consequence might be to say, "For every minute you are late, we will set your alarm clock that many minutes earlier tomorrow, so you will be able to be ready on time."

A child hits another child.

Punishment might be to say, "You are a bad boy! 10 minutes in time out!"

Consequence might be to say, "I see you are angry at her! You may tell her why you are angry by saying 'It made me mad when you took my truck!' but you *may not* hit. If you hit again you will have to play over there by yourself." (Notice that the consequence teaches what *to* do to replace the unacceptable behavior.)

Punishment focuses on the failure of the child. Consequence focuses on how to improve.

I should mention here that I consider bribery or rewards to be just the other side of the punishment coin. If you entice a child to a certain behavior with rewards, and she strives to do well with the reward as her goal, then you are distracting her from her own natural inner reward, the pride she'll feel in knowing that she did her best. If she is accustomed to this inner reward, then she will strive to do her best whether there is a material bribe or not. So you must ask yourself, are you willing to be there to offer her rewards for the rest of her life? Research shows that rewards decrease intrinsic (inner) motivation.

Exercise Nineteen

SOME POINTS OF VIEW ON PUNISHMENT

"Power is of two kinds. One is obtained by fear of punishment, and the other by acts of love. Power based on love is a thousand times more effective and permanent than the one derived from fear of punishment."
—*Gandhi*

Elizabeth Gershoff, a developmental psychologist with Columbia University's National Center for Children in Poverty, conducted what many researchers consider the most comprehensive study on spanking.

The study found children who were spanked most often were the most likely to exhibit one or more of 11 negative behaviors, which included everything from depression to later abuse of one's own child or spouse.

"The more children are spanked the more likely they are to be aggressive, delinquent, defiant, to have mental health issues in the future and to have more relationship issues with the parent," Gershoff says.

"All actual punishment, I shall consider superfluous, and even harmful.
If damage has been done it should be made good by the children.
If naughtiness persists in the class as a whole, the teachers may well seek the fault within themselves."
- Rudolf Steiner

"When adults rely regularly on rewards and punishments, children come to depend on the judgment of others as the basis for their own moral decisions. Rewards and punishments create 'other control'. Children grow up focusing on what others demand of them and what they in turn will demand from others."

"Consequences help children think about the effects of their choices and draw conclusions about the wisdom of those choices. This builds responsibility - the ability to respond appropriately to situations."
—Becky Goldman, *Easy to Love, Difficult to Discipline*

Exercise Twenty

MORE POINTS OF VIEW ON PUNISHMENT

"From a review of the literature it is concluded that physical punishment by parents does not inhibit violence and most likely encourages it. Punishment both frustrates the child and gives him a model to learn from."
—Committee on Violence, Dept. of Psychiatry,
Stanford U., *Violence and the Struggle for Existence*

"Punishment can be discarded forever in disciplining children. And I mean all kinds of punishment, not just the physical kind. Parents can raise children who are responsible, self disciplined and cooperative without relying on the weapon of fear. They can learn how to influence children to behave out of genuine consideration for the needs of parents, rather than out of fear of punishment or withdrawal of privileges."
—Dr. Thomas Gordon, *Parent Effectiveness Training*

Where did we ever get the crazy idea that in order to make children perform better, we must first make them feel worse?
This power to impose suffering is a common mistake made by many parents and teachers - so much so that they often lose sight of their primary goal of inspiring children to improve their behavior...   Parents and teachers also don't like to admit that punishment can feel good to them because it gives them the sense of power they feel is being taken away from them when children misbehave. This, of course, is not part of their conscious awareness, but when confronted with it they usually recognize it.
In rational moments, adults know that their bottom-line goal is to inspire children to be happy, responsible people. However, it is so easy to get lost in pride and ego goals.
Ineffective behavior on the part of adults is not always based on pride and ego. Sometimes they are honestly misguided. Many believe that punishment is the best way to motivate children to do better. They really believe that

in order to make children do better, they first have to make them feel worse.
—Jane Nelsen, Ed.D, Positive Discipline

Schools are the breeding grounds for our society's negative subcultures. Schools do not intend to hurt children, but like much of the rest of our society they often respond to wrongdoing with punishment. They operate under the false expectation that punishment causes children to change their ways.

The result of all those punitive writing assignments, detentions, suspensions and expulsions is a growing number of young people who see themselves as outcasts, as "bad." School disciplinary procedures, as in the criminal justice system, provide little or no opportunity for reintegration - for making amends, apologizing, repairing the harm or shedding the offender label. They exclude from the disciplinary process those most affected by the offense - the offenders, victims and their respective communities of care. The primary difference between schools and courts is that schools start alienating offenders at an earlier age.
—Ted Wachtel, Real Justice

Exercise Twenty One

CREATING CONSEQUENCES

Creating consequences is a true art form.

It's difficult enough when all is calm and serene, but when we are trying to accomplish this creative act while two kids are at each other's throats, or when we are standing in a crowded restaurant with a screaming child, the task becomes monumental.

I hope by doing the exercises in this book, you will get more skillful, and will be able to come up with appropriate consequences even in the midst of chaos.

IT ISN'T NECESSARY FOR A CHILD TO SUFFER IN ORDER TO LEARN

Sometimes consequences will be uncomfortable for a child; he may have to do something he'd rather not do, and doesn't enjoy. Other times the child may not mind at all.

If you find yourself caring whether the child suffers or not, then you may still be in the punishment mode. See if you can switch your focus to teaching the child, and see if you can accomplish this teaching without the child suffering. That would be ideal, no? If you believe that he must suffer to learn, then your "consequences" are really punishments.

"Boys! Grandma is sleeping and your noise is liable to wake her up."
Ten minutes later: "Boys! I reminded you that Grandma is sleeping yet you seem to be unable to remember to keep your voices down. Go on up to your rooms and play there until she awakes."

Some people would say that this discipline would be ineffective if the boys liked to play in their rooms. They'd say that it wouldn't "teach" the boys anything unless the "consequence" made them suffer. These boys may or may not enjoy playing in their rooms. But the point isn't to make them suffer. The point is to say, "If you can't keep your own noise level down, the logical consequence will be to send you away." It isn't about them being "bad." It's about them learning the skill of considering other people's needs.

CONSEQUENCES SHOULD BE RELATED TO THE BEHAVIOR

"You forgot your homework again? No dessert tonight!" This is a punishment. The dessert has nothing to do with the homework.

Consequences might be that she must show you that she has her homework materials before getting in the car every day.

CONSEQUENCES ARE DESIGNED TO TEACH THE CHILD ABOUT THE NATURAL LAW OF THE WORLD

If you make too much noise, or do things that annoy people, they won't want to be around you.

If you make a mess, you are expected to clean it up.

If you forget to do something, there are consequences for you later - the job won't be done when it needs to be.

If you act in an untrustworthy way, people will no longer trust you and will take precautions against your behavior.

If you don't respect other people's property, they won't want to lend you things. If you don't respect your own property, it will no longer function to serve you.

These things are obvious to us, but to our children they may not be. These are the kinds of things we are trying to teach them.

When punishments are given that serve only to make the child suffer, the opportunity to teach these truths is lost.

"The last time I let you use my CD's you left them out of their cases. Now I don't want to let you use them today." This is a logical consequence.

"You left my CD's out. No allowance this week." This is a punishment.

CONSEQUENCES TEACH THE CHILD HOW TO MAKE AMENDS FOR HIS MISTAKES

"You thought it was funny to put paint on his shirt. But now you must buy him a new shirt with your own money." This is a consequence.

"You are grounded" is a punishment.

CONSEQUENCES NEED TO BE IMPLEMENTABLE. EMPTY THREATS ARE EMPTY.

"Leia, put that down right now or I'm taking you home!" Leia looks at Dad, and just laughs; she knows he won't follow through with that threat.

Better for him to have said, "Leia, put that down or I'll pick you up and keep you on my lap." This is a much milder threat, but a real one.

Don't threaten something unless you are willing and able to do it.

Exercise Twenty Two

PUNISHMENT VS. CONSEQUENCES EXERCISES

For each of the following situations, come up with a punishment and a consequence.

Remember to ask yourself whether the consequence is:

A. Related to the misbehavior

B. Teaches the child about the natural laws of the world

C. Teaches the child how to make amends for the mistake

D. Is something that YOU can and are willing to implement

E. Is proportional to the severity of the misbehavior

1. 2 year old Brian grabs food off his brother's plate.

_____

_____

_____

_____

_____

_____

_____

2. 3 year old Marsha won't put on her dress because she wants to wear her new bathing suit to school.

_____

_____

_____

_____

_____

_____

_____

3. 4 year old Jenny hits a little boy next to her.

_____

_____

_____

_____

_____

_____

4. 5 year old Kamal played the piano at 6:00 in the morning on Sunday, waking up his teenage sister.

_____

_____

_____

_____

_____

_____

These questions are about young children. For children older than 6 years, you can use the How to Feel Nice With All Folks acronym to help the child resolve conflict and make amends himself. See Exercise Thirty Seven, The Art of Refereeing.

ANSWERS:

1. Brian just doesn't know how to be polite yet. A punishment might be to yell at him, or slap his hand, or show anger. A consequence might be to remove the food from Brian's hand, look him kindly in the eyes and say, "This is your brother's food. It's not OK to take it off his plate. Here is some for you from the serving dish."

2. Marsha is obviously excited about her new bathing suit. Although you may feel frustrated and angry with her for not "listening to you," you need to also look at what is happening inside of her. Punishment might be "Put this dress on or I'm going to take back your bathing suit," or taking away something she likes, or putting her in a time out.

    Consequences might look like "Marsha, I see that you really like your bathing suit. That's wonderful! I wish you could wear it to school. And even wear it to bed! And to the bathtub too! And wear it every single minute of every day until you are all grown up! (silliness, helping her to know that you are understanding and honoring her wishes). But unfortunately, you aren't allowed to wear bathing suits to school. So let's put it here on your bed and as soon as you get home from school you can change into it."

    Or, you can offer "You aren't allowed to just wear a bathing suit, but you can wear it under your dress."

    And if Marsha is still not cooperating, your consequence might be more severe; you might say, "Marsha I'm sorry you are sad about not being able to wear your bathing suit, but the school doesn't allow it. We have to go now or we'll be late. I'm not going to fight with you. You either let me put this dress on you right now, or I'm going to pick you up with nothing on and put you in the car, and you'll have to get dressed when we get to school."

3. Punishment for Jenny might be to hit her (which really doesn't make much sense, since you are trying to teach her that hitting isn't OK), or to put her in time out, or to yell at her.

    Consequences might be to look her in the eyes, explain, "Jenny when you hit the boy it hurt him. That's not OK." Show her what she should have done instead to meet whatever need she was trying to meet. And pick her up and move her to her own space, explaining that you are moving her to protect the boy. This may seem similar to time out, but there is a difference in feeling nature between the two. To put her in time out in order to cause her suffering with the belief that this will prevent her from hitting anymore would be to punish. To just move her for the purpose of protecting the boy is a consequence. The point isn't to make her suffer; it is to protect the boy.

4. Kamal is a bit young to be able to remember not to play, so consequences might be geared toward helping him remember. You can close the piano keyboard cover each night, and Kamal can then be told to ask before opening it. Or his sister can open it for him when she wakes. This is treating Kamal as just a small person without grownup skills to remember, and helping him to learn these skills. Seeing him as "bad" might make you inclined to punish him, remove his piano playing privileges, or take away his dessert or allowance. To teach him to take responsibility for his mistakes, you can suggest nice things he could do for his sister - make her breakfast, or offer to clean up her dishes from breakfast, etc. This will keep good relations between the children, and help to build Kamal's self-esteem.

Exercise Twenty Three

PUTTING IT ALL TOGETHER

NEEDS / OK WANTS / NOT OK WANTS / AND RESPONSES

Putting together everything we've discussed so far – when you encounter a situation with your child where he is making a request or behaving in an unacceptable manner, keep in mind the concept of wants vs. needs, knowing when to say Yes and when to say No, in order to keep in the center of the Boot Camp - Mayhem Continuum. This means to consider both the needs of the child and the needs of others. And if it is necessary to say No, how to do so in a way that will create a consequence that teaches.

For the following, identify:

1. The need
2. The Not Ok Want, being sure to specify how satisfying the want would hurt other people, the environment, or the child's future self.
3. And devise an appropriate response.

1. 4 year old Zack, sitting in an auditorium during an adult lecture, begins to jump up and down in his seat after sitting quietly for 20 minutes.

Need: _____

Not OK want: _____

Response: _____

2. You are on the phone, and your 6 year old daughter Nora marches

into the kitchen and announces "I need scrambled eggs right now!"

Need: _____

Not OK want: _____

Response: _____

3. Your 11 year old son Christopher and his four friends want to ride their bikes to the movies. They must cross a highway near your home to get there.

Need: _____

Not OK want: _____

Response: _____

4. Your 8 year old daughter Samantha wants to go with a friend and her parents overnight on a trip, but you're not comfortable because you don't know the parents.

Need: _____

Not OK want: _____

Response: _____

5. 5 year old Mark dislikes healthy food and wants to eat sugar cereal for dinner.

Need: _____

Not OK want: _____

Response: _____

6. You are speaking to another adult and your 9 year old daughter Cathy interrupts you.

Need: _____

Not OK want: _____

Response: _____

7. It's bedtime and your 4 year old Alex doesn't want to go to bed.

Need: _____

Not OK want: _____

Response: _____

8. Your 16 year old Liza wants to try out her brand new drivers permit on a busy road.

Need: _____

Not OK want: _____

Response: _____

PUTTING IT ALL TOGETHER

ANSWERS:

1. Need- Zack, like any small boy, needs to release his excess energy through movement. His jumping isn't an attempt to be "bad"; it's just an attempt to feel OK.

   Not OK Want – Zack's jumping would disturb other people in the lecture.

   Response – You could give him the option to sit quietly, offer him a quiet toy to use, or if he is very uncomfortable, bring him outside for a race around the outside of the building to expend his energy.

2. Need – Nora needs to eat.

   Not OK Want – The demand for eggs right now would force you to prematurely end your phone call.

   Response – You could give her the option to get cereal for herself now or wait until you are off the phone to help her make eggs.

3. Need - Christopher needs to try out his skills in the world and explore. He needs to work towards competence and autonomy and have adventure.

   Not OK Want – The risk to life and limb of crossing a highway may be too much.

   Response – You could suggest a safer destination, or that you will drive them to the movies, and they can go in by themselves, or that you will drop them and their bikes off across the highway and they could ride from there.

4. Need – Samantha needs to socialize, to belong to society.

Not Ok Want – You feel she might not be safe.

Response – You can offer just play dates until you get to know the parents. Or you can phone the parents.

5. Need – Although you are conscious of Mark's need to eat healthy food, he is expressing the conflicting need to listen to his body's voice of what appeals to him and also the need for pleasure in life. If too much sugar is available, his body's voice may become confused by the addiction.

   Not OK Want – He wants to feed his addiction, which is unhealthy.

   Response – You can refrain from buying the foods you don't want him to eat, and allow him full choice of healthy foods. Then he will eat sugar only occasionally.

6. Need – Cathy needs you to be available to speak with her.

   Not OK Want – She doesn't need to speak to you immediately – she can learn patience.

   Response – You can ask her if there is an emergency – if she responds in the negative, then inform her "Cathy, I am in the middle of a conversation right now, you may say 'excuse me' and then wait until I am free to speak to you."

7. Need – Alex needs fun!

   Not Ok Want – He doesn't need fun every minute. He doesn't *need* fun right now.

   Response – You can say "I know it's hard to go to bed when you are having fun," as you carry him up to bed.

8. Need – Liza needs to learn to drive in order to develop competence and autonomy.

   Not Ok Want – She doesn't need to practice in a dangerous place.

   Response – Sometimes, though hopefully not often, you will need to just say no to your teen. She is still in the developmental stages of making good life decisions, so sometimes when her "mistakes" might endanger her life, you will need to act from a place of authority. But in the best of circumstances, at this age, these times will be few and far between. Of course, along with your "no" you'd provide an explanation as to why.

Exercise Twenty Four

THE ART OF SAYING NO

ICE

I — Inform

C — State Consequence

E — Enact

Once you have distinguished needs, and OK wants, from Not OK wants, and you've decided to say "No", you can use the following process to help you to do so without blame, punishment, negativity, insensitivity, and also without wimping out.

This should be a temporary system, which you can use to help you move you from a current unhealthy relationship or habitual way of interacting with your children into a healthier one. Once this new way is in place (usually in no more than two weeks), there should be almost no friction between you and your children. Children are social beings and given a kind, self-assured adult to lead them, they will want to cooperate.

There should be no need for force.

I used to believe the typical negative expectations about the "normal" horrors of the terrible two's, the teenage years, etc. But now I see that they are only "normal" in our society because they are very common, not because they are natural or inevitable. It is by no means natural to our species, and I don't believe it is necessary for children to have a constant battle of the wills with their parents at any stage of their lives.

In this exercise I describe a simple system of discipline using the acronym I.C.E. This I.C.E. system is applicable mostly to young children. Past the age of 7 or so, you would want to move into a bit more dialogue, as set forth in the upcoming exercise on "Refereeing."

Once you have gone through the process of determining that the current desire of your child is *not* a need, and that it is a desire that is *not ok* with you, then you can proceed as follows:

Just remember the acronym ICE.
(Ice is helpful to cool off a hot situation...)

I is for inform:

In a simple sentence, inform your child what he must do,
"It's time for bed. Pick up your toys now."

or what he must stop doing,
"It's not OK to scream that loud here. Lower your voice please."

There really is no reason to ask your child any questions here, such as, "Are you ready for bed yet?" His inclinations shouldn't be relevant at this stage since you have already considered them and made a decision.

C is for choice:

COMPLIANCE
"You can pick up your toys now" Or offer a wider choice - "You

can pick up your toys now, or after you get a drink."
OR
CONSEQUENCE
"Or I will _____".
See note below about Consequences.

E is for enact:

You quietly carry out the consequence from above. There is no need at this point for you to say any more.

Two notes about consequences:

1. I once heard a little boy say, "I was bad and my consequence is no dessert." A punishment by any other name is still a punishment.

2. Please note that you cannot *make* your child do anything. You can only make *yourself* do something. So when creating consequences, remember to state what *you* will do. "I will escort you to your room." "I will pick up the toys and put them away in the attic for a week."

This ICE method requires a little memorization.

I is for _____

C is for _____

E is for _____

Exercise Twenty Five

THE EXITS

There are three exits to the above discipline pathway. They are labeled I.C.E. also, since most of us have rather limited memories. Each exit has an "E" activity associated with it.

I is for new Information:

If, in the process of doing the above I.C.E. discipline transaction, you discover new information ("But Daddy, I'm hungry, I didn't eat lunch today!), then you might want to exit the I.C.E. transaction and once again enter the entire process from the beginning, rethinking whether this is a need, an OK want, or still a NOT OK want. It's OK if your child sees you make a mistake and change directions. This will model flexibility, which is a useful trait for your child to develop.

C is for comply:

Obviously, if your child complies, then you are done. If you like, you can encourage any positive behavior as you exit the transaction.

"I see you've chosen to pick up your toys. Fantastic!" or

"Thank you for lowering your voice. I can hear my phone call much better now and I really appreciate it."

It is more helpful to direct your comments to the *action* taken, rather than to the person. "What a great job!" rather than "What a good boy!"

E is for emotional outburst:

Don't let this really be an exit. Just make it a temporary detour.

If your child has a strong emotional reaction, you can empathize with the child so he can feel understood. If possible, put your arms around him so he can feel your love. And help to verbalize what he might be experiencing. "I see that you are having such a good time with this toy and you probably really want to keep playing, right? And I know that it is hard to stop playing when you are having so much fun."

Then allow the emotions to be expressed:

If he's crying, just hold the child and rock and kiss him. Let him cry until you ask if there are any more tears left and he says no.

If it's anger, help direct the expression of it to a way that doesn't hurt anyone else or himself - you can cross your arms and stomp your feet and say "You must feel *mad!*" or if there's a lot of aggression, direct him to pummel a pillow, or to use his voice "Let's say, '*I'm Mad!*' as loud as we can!" When his energy level comes down, you can move on.

A quick note about "brattiness." If you feel the urge to use this label, see if you can stop for a second, and look into the eyes of the child. Often what I see in so-called bratty children is a very frightened child. Remember, they aren't yet old enough to distinguish between a want and a need. When they were infants, their wants were needs. And up until now, their parents responded to their wants and needs in the same way. Now all of a sudden, the rug is pulled out from under them. Their power to get their needs/wants met doesn't seem to be working! This does not feel OK! It can actually feel life threatening. With this perspective it is a little easier to understand why a child would get so frantic about not getting what seems like such a silly whim fulfilled. It can be very helpful at this point to address this concern with your child. Assure him that he doesn't *need* this desire to be fulfilled. Let him know that he will be fine without it. Just verbalizing "It's OK to not get what you want all the time. You'll be fine. I will make sure you get your needs filled. Don't worry" can totally relax a child and end the brat attack.

The key here is to accept the emotions of the child.

If this is difficult for you, then perhaps you would benefit from doing some work to become more comfortable with your own emotions. See the next exercise for some hints.

Then when the child is back in a calm state, restate the choice (see above) and continue the transaction. It's OK for a child to express his emotions, but it isn't OK to use that expression to get out of the transaction.

Exercise Twenty Six

MEMORIZE THE EXITS TOO

The "E" activity when you are exiting is:

If you get new Information, E is for

_____

If your child Complies, E is for

_____

If your child has an Emotional outburst, E is for

_____

Exercise Twenty Seven through Thirty Four

USING ICE

The exercise for today is to take one discipline situation and fill in the blanks below to show one way it could have happened according to ICE:

I nform

_____

Write what you could have said

C hoice

_____

Write what complying looks like and a consequence
if they don't comply

E nact

_____

Imagine yourself enacting the consequence

Now imagine the 3 exits:
I nformation

_____

Write some new information that you might have received which
would cause you to reENTER the decision making process

C omply

_____

Imagine your child complying, and write an ENCOURAGEMENT
here

E motional Outburst

_____

Imagine your child having a fit and imagine how you'd like
to react with EMPATHY.

_____

Write an empathic statement here.

Then imagine your child calming down, and you restating his choice, as above.

I strongly suggest doing this imaginal exercise daily for a week. Practice makes perfect, and imagining counts as practice

Exercise Thirty Five

EMOTIONAL OUTBURSTS

As parents we have to deal with emotional outbursts from two sources; our children and ourselves. Learning how to deal with our own emotional outbursts gives us skills that enable us to handle our kids' emotions in a healthy way.

A thorough discussion of how to process emotions takes a whole book in itself. See my book Emotions – An Owner's Manual. But here I will try to impart one basic skill.

In my workshops, parents often say that they know what they "should" do in difficult discipline situations; they aren't confused or unsure in their understanding of wants vs. needs or in how to say no. But, unfortunately, a strange phenomenon sometimes occurs, where all of a sudden they find that they have been possessed! A demon or a witch has come into their body! And it yells at their kids! Through no fault of their own! I believe that this phenomenon isn't limited to just a psychotic few. When someone in a workshop is brave enough to admit it out loud, the rest of the participants, it appears, can relate deeply, and their laughter betrays that they have had a similar experience.

This experience, of feeling possessed, is a natural biological reaction to stress. When the parent encounters a child or children behaving in a way which causes alarm, the parent's brain goes into survival mode. The part of our brain activated in times of stress is the hindbrain, the reptilian brain, which we have in common with all animals. We are biologically wired, when in danger, to act automatically according to the instincts of this part of our brain. When this is happening, we are unable to use the higher part of our brain, our neocortex, or thinking brain. This is why it feels to us as if a demon has possessed us. All of a sudden, we find ourselves acting in ways that we never would consciously choose to act.

EXORCISING THE DEMON

How can we best deal with these times of intense emotion?
Here is a five step process:

1. BECOME AWARE OF THE EMOTION

First you will need to become aware on a conscious level of the strong emotion in your body. You have about a quarter of a second from the time the emotion arises until the initiation of the automatic reaction, in which to stop the process. It takes practice to notice the emotion in time. You can increase your ability to do this by spending 10 minutes daily just thinking through your day and noticing the physical sensation of your emotions in your body as you remember your day. This will help you to become more aware of your emotions. And then when they arise, you will be more able to notice them on the spot.

This is the hardest part of the process because our instincts tell us to react immediately to the emotion with physical action. So we have to learn to go against this deeply ingrained habit. It is ingrained not only in our own lives, but in our species as well. It may take time to be able to accomplish this, so have patience with yourself.

Even if you are in mid-screech when you suddenly realize that you have been possessed, that is OK. Just apologize, say "give me a second", and continue on with this process.

2. CONCENTRATE ON THE PHYSICAL SENSATION OF THE EMOTION IN YOUR BODY

Second, you need to give yourself a time out. Just stop whatever you're doing, and discharge the intense emotion from your body. Once the emotion is discharged, you will be able to activate your neocortex again and make an intelligent, rational decision about the best course of action to take. To discharge the emotion try following these 3 steps:

A. Close your eyes. Helpful but not essential. It's especially helpful when you are just learning this new skill.

B. Take 3 full breaths. Fill your belly. Then fill your chest. Then let go. Repeat 3 times.

C. Focus your attention onto the physical sensations of the emotion in your body.

I know this sounds too simple to be helpful. But it is not as simple as it sounds. This is based on Buddhist psychology and it is very powerful. Actually describe to yourself what the sensations are -

1) Where do you feel the sensation? In your belly? Your chest? Your hands? Behind your eyes? Your legs? Be as clear as you can in your description. "I feel a sensation starting from my solar plexus and going up to my throat."

2) What is the quality of the sensation? Is it hot? Cold? A tightness? Fluttery? Dull? An emptiness? A tingling? Numbness? What object might it remind you of? If it had a color what color would it be?

3) How intense is the sensation? Notice how strongly you feel it. Assign a number from one to ten to indicate how intense it is.

3. BREATHE INTO THE SENSATION

Next, while you are continuing to focus your attention on the physical sensation in your body, begin to aim your breath into the area of the sensation. Continue to breathe fully, as above, full belly, full chest, let go.

4. WATCH THE CHANGE IN THE SENSATION

Doing this technique will allow the emotion to move. At first, the emotion might even seem to grow inside you. Don't be discouraged. Just allow it full rein to move and change as it wishes. Your job is to simply watch it. Watch it with equanimity. Don't try to make it do anything.

Just give it your full attention, but don't make any effort to stop, move, or change it in any way. Fully breathing into the sensation, become aware of any changes. Does the sensation dissipate? Or become more intense? Or change qualities? Or move to a different part of your body? Whatever it does, just notice it.

Intense sadness may want to discharge through tears. Despite the fact that society doesn't usually condone crying, this is the way nature intended us to discharge this energy. Anger wants to discharge through muscular activity. It doesn't have to be hitting someone else! It can simply be through tensing the muscles. Or if the option is available to you, pummel some pillows, or scream in your car.

If you continue doing this technique, the emotion will eventually pass through you. That's just the nature of emotions. They move. They pass. Have you ever known anyone to stay angry or sad or afraid for a month? No! Emotions come and go. Breathing helps this movement to happen.

5. TURN ON YOUR BRAIN

When you feel that the intensity of the emotion, the energy of the feeling, has left your body through your breath, then you have discharged the emotion and are ready to engage your logical thinking brain. Then you will be in a position to apply the understanding you have gained from reading this book.

BECOMING COMFORTABLE WITH EMOTION

The above is a high level meditative practice. It's not easy. It puts you in the place of "witness." This is utilizing and activating the highest evolutionary part of your brain, the frontal lobes. It is this part of the brain that is active, and measurable, during the meditation of yogis. It is the seat of our spiritual experience and capacity. By activating the frontal lobes, you are pulling yourself out of the lower modules of your brain. You are no longer at the beck and call of the reptilian and old mammalian parts of your brain. Though the instincts are still there available to you, you are activating your uniquely human capacity, which is to be able to choose your action, to decide consciously whether or not to act on those instinctive impulses.

The idea is to become comfortable allowing a full range of emotional flow, while still staying connected and centered on your breath. You can learn to allow your entire being to be filled with anger (also known as power) while retaining equanimity and a deep calm. You can feel safe entering into deep sadness, letting your heart open and soften, becoming compassionate for all beings. You can let the feeling sensations of fear just pass through your body, without ruffling your feathers.

The more you can acquire this equanimity with your own emotions, the more you will be able to retain equanimity while your child expresses his emotions.

PRACTICE THIS TECHNIQUE

Here is a way to practice this technique so that during the heat of a situation you will have some skill under your belt.

1. Close your eyes. Put your feet on the floor, or lie on a bed. Breathe fully; full belly, full chest, let go.

2. Recall an emotional incident. Replay in your mind the circumstances. Recall the visuals, as well as the sounds, the smells, and the feel of the situation.

3. Now the physical sensation of that emotion should be in your body. You can now practice the technique outlined above.

BECOMING COMFORTABLE WITH YOUR CHILD'S EMOTIONS

Any negative emotion that is not fully faced and seen for what it is in the moment it arises does not completely dissolve. It leaves behind a remnant of pain.

Children in particular find strong negative emotions too overwhelming to cope with and tend to try not to feel them. In the absence of a fully conscious adult who guides them with love and compassionate understanding into facing the emotion directly, choosing not to feel it is indeed the only option for the child at that time. Unfortunately, that early defense mechanism usually remains in place when the child becomes an adult. The emotion still lives in him or her unrecognized and manifests indirectly, for example, as anxiety, anger, outbursts of violence, a mood, or even as a physical illness. In some cases, it interferes with or sabotages every intimate relationship.

The remnants of pain left behind by every strong negative emotion that is not fully faced, accepted, and then let go of join together to form an energy field that lives in the very cells of your body. . . . This energy field of old but still very-much-alive emotion that lives in almost every human being is the pain-body.
Eckhart Tolle, A New Earth

One problem that many parents encounter is that when their child expresses emotion, they become so uncomfortable with this expression that they have an emotional reaction themselves. Then they have two emotional outbursts to deal with at once.

The technique needed to deal with your child's emotions is the same one described above for dealing with your own. Simply find your own breath, and breathe fully in your own body. Let your own emotional reaction just flow out with your outbreath. Just stay still and calm and allow the emotional flow through your child as if it were an emotion flowing through your own body. In the same way you'd work with an emotion in your own body, pay full attention, but don't butt in! Be there to prevent damage to self and property. Be there to provide warm loving hugs if they are asked for. But otherwise be OK just waiting with patience. Know that the expression will soon end.

Find that place inside you of OK'ness. If you can stay in that place, you will convey to your child just what she is needing. She will gain that inner sense of calm about life. She will see that though emotions come and go, that it's OK. They are only temporary. You can retain equanimity even during the flow of emotion. You are essentially serving as the child's ego during her emotional flows. As she grows and develops her own ego, she will model this calmness. She will model this skill, of allowing a full flow of emotion, while retaining equanimity within her own ego. What a gift to give a child!

Exercise Thirty Six

DEEP PREPARATION FOR THE NO BLAME APPROACH

If you are a poetry hater, skip this exercise. For the rest of us, I find Kahlil Gibran's treatise on punishment to be extremely healing. It promotes a deep acceptance of all people. I believe that it is only from this place of acceptance and love that true healing can take place.

Then one of the judges of the city stood forth and said,
Speak to us of Crime and Punishment.
And he answered, saying:
It is when your spirit goes wandering upon the wind,
That you, alone and unguarded, commit a wrong unto others and therefore unto yourself.
And for that wrong committed must you knock and wait a while unheeded at the gate of the blessed.

Like the ocean is your god-self;
It remains for ever undefiled.
And like the ether it lifts but the winged.
Even like the sun is your god-self;
It knows not the ways of the mole nor seeks it the holes of the serpent.
But your god-self dwells not alone in your being.
Much in you is still man, and much in you is not yet man,
But a shapeless pigmy that walks asleep in the mist searching for its own awakening.
And of the man in you would I now speak.
For it is he and not your god-self nor the pigmy in the mist, that knows crime and the punishment of crime.

Oftentimes have I heard you speak of one who commits a wrong as though he were not one of you, but a stranger unto you and an intruder upon your world.

But I say that even as the holy and the righteous cannot rise beyond the highest which is in each one of you,

So the wicked and the weak cannot fall lower than the lowest which is in you also.

And as a single leaf turns not yellow but with the silent knowledge of the whole tree,

So the wrong-doer cannot do wrong without the hidden will of you all.

Like a procession you walk together towards your god-self.

You are the way and the wayfarers.

And when one of you falls down he falls for those behind him, a caution against the stumbling stone.

Ay, and he falls for those ahead of him, who though faster and surer of foot, yet removed not the stumbling stone.

And this also, though the word lie heavy upon your hearts;

The murdered is not unaccountable for his own murder,

And the robbed is not blameless in being robbed.

The righteous is not innocent of the deeds of the wicked,

And the white-handed is not clean in the doings of the felon.

Yea, the guilty is oftentimes the victim of the injured,

And still more often the condemned is the burden bearer for the guiltless and unblamed.

You cannot separate the just from the unjust and the good from the wicked;

For they stand together before the face of the sun even as the black thread and the white are woven together.

And when the black thread breaks, the weaver shall look into the whole cloth, and he shall examine the loom also.

If any of you would bring to judgment the unfaithful wife,
Let him also weigh the heart of her husband in scales, and measure his soul with measurements.
And let him who would lash the offender look unto the spirit of the offended.
And if any of you would punish in the name of righteousness and lay the ax unto the evil tree, let him see to its roots;
And verily he will find the roots of the good and the bad, the fruitful and the fruitless, all entwined together in the silent heart of the earth.
And you judges who would be just,
What judgment pronounce you upon him who though honest in the flesh yet is a thief in spirit?
What penalty lay you upon him who slays in the flesh yet is himself slain in the spirit?
And how prosecute you him who in action is a deceiver and an oppressor,
Yet who also is aggrieved and outraged?

And how shall you punish those whose remorse is already greater than their misdeeds?
Is not remorse the justice which is administered by that very law which you would fain serve?
Yet you cannot lay remorse upon the innocent nor lift it from the heart of the guilty.
Unbidden shall it call in the night, that men may wake and gaze upon themselves.
And you who would understand justice, how shall you unless you look upon all deeds in the fullness of light?
Only then shall you know that the erect and the fallen are but one man standing in twilight between the night of his pigmy-self and the day of his god-self,
And that the corner-stone of the temple is not higher than the lowest stone in its foundation.

—Kahlil Gibran, The Prophet

Exercise Thirty Seven

THE ART OF REFEREEING

A/K/A: HELPING KIDS PRACTICE CONFLICT RESOLUTION

The Acronym I.C.E. is useful for parenting young children (under age 7) who are well served by being parented with authority. This is putting your child on a tricycle. But it certainly is inappropriate for teenagers who would consider such an approach to be insulting, and indeed it would be. They would rebel against it (at least I hope they would) and in fact, that is what I see happening with several of my daughter's high school friends and their parents.

For older children you can start to bring in more dialogue. You will want to move gradually (training wheels) toward a dialoguing method of conflict resolution. First, I'll present the dialogue as it is used with adults and children over approximately 10 years. Then I'll suggest how you might modify it to be appropriate for children 7-10 years old.

This dialogue makes use of six basic principles common to almost all conflict resolution methods, whether it be Restorative Justice in the court system, peer mediation in high schools, the Path program in elementary schools, Coach4Success tm in businesses, or professional mediation. These six simple elements are:

1. TELLING THE STORY

Both parties tell their side of the story so that differences in point of view can become apparent. An old East Indian parable helps explain the reason this element is so important. Five blind men went to "see" an elephant. The first man, positioned on the side of the elephant, said, "An elephant is like a wall." The second man, positioned at the tail said, "An elephant is like a rope." The third man, positioned at the trunk said,

"I believe you two are mistaken. An elephant is like a hose." The fourth man, feeling the leg, said, "Are you all kidding around with me? An elephant is obviously like a tree trunk." And the fifth, feeling the ears, said, "Are you all crazy? Surely an elephant is like a fan."

For a relationship to function smoothly, and without tension, it is extremely helpful if all parties can agree that although objective reality exists, it isn't something we can know for sure. What we can know is our own point of view. We can also know how we feel, what we believe, and our own motivations. We can communicate these, as best we can, to each other. So in the first element, of telling the story, it is important, as referee, to be conscious of the language used. Be sure that what is being reported *could have been videotaped*. Be sure the child is telling just the physical aspects of what happened and is refraining from adding his own subjective feelings or beliefs, or from stating as objective reality what the other person's subjective feelings, motivations or beliefs were.

Ask him to rephrase "Christopher was trying to make Sarah cry by taking her book. He's so mean." to just say "I saw Christopher take a book off Sarah's desk." The physical action of Christopher taking the book off Sarah's desk can be videotaped. Christopher's motivation (trying to make Sarah cry) is not videotapeable. It is the speaker's assumption about Christopher's motivation. Christopher "being mean" is, of course, not videotapeable either. What does "being mean" look like?

This first step, of just clarifying the point of view of both parties, is very often all that is needed to resolve the conflict.

"No, I took *my* book off of Sarah's desk."

2. COMMUNICATING FEELINGS

In the second step, dropping down from the level of "what happened," into the level of feelings, the parties in conflict reveal the vulnerable human side of themselves.

When we are in conflict, our bodies become flooded with a defensive hormonal cocktail of cortisol and adrenalin, which indicates that the part of the brain which is activated is the reptilian brain. This is the part of the brain which is responsible for our survival. When the reptilian brain is strongly activated, the higher brain functions are temporarily suspended. A person concerned with his own survival, who is in this defensive mode, is not aware of the other person except as a "dangerous object." The other person is objectified and dehumanized.

When, during a dialogue, the parties take the time to hear the feelings of the other person, they can once again become aware of the human side of him. He is no longer just a "prop" in the play of life.

We are biologically wired to care about each other. Even babies, when shown a picture of someone in pain, are motivated to try to help. Often this awareness of the other person's pain and the desire to help him is the main motivating force towards change. This bears repeating - because of our biological wiring, our herd and nurturing instincts, a person is more likely to be motivated towards personal change by wanting to ease the pain of others, than he would be by bribe or punishment. This is why this step of revealing feelings is so crucial.

Often, young children are not even aware of the effect their actions have on others. By hearing the expression of the painful feelings they have unintentionally caused, they can learn very quickly and directly to consider others.

3. IDENTIFYING THE POSITIVE MOTIVATION

This step helps us to move from shame to self-esteem. The validation of the intrinsic goodness of each person and the honoring of their right to try to fulfill their needs is an incredibly important step in helping us avoid judgment and the infliction of psychological wounds.

Identifying the need is the first step towards finding a way to meet the need in a better way. If the need isn't identified, the focus remains on how to change the errant behavior. But if the need which is motivating that behavior is still unmet, the behavior is likely to recur, no matter how much the child is punished, because it is human to try to fulfill one's needs. Be sure you are identifying bare naked needs, which are usually one word, like 'belonging' or 'safety.' It is essential that you unhook the needs from the strategies to meet them.

4. BRAINSTORMING A SOLUTION

The purpose of this step is to move the relationship from a combative, conflictual one to a partnership where the two sides work together towards a mutually satisfying resolution of the conflict. This means that you are searching for strategies that meet all needs. This provides better results because:

a. Two heads are better than one.

b. Since no one is attacking, no one needs to act defensively. Energies which might have gone towards defensive maneuvers that actually work against mutual resolution are now freed up to be used to work towards a positive goal.

c. When a child has taken a part in creating the solution to a problem, then the motivation to follow through is coming from within and enforcement will no longer be an issue (although keep in mind that since they are still in the process of developing their life skills, support may still be necessary).

d. Once a child is old enough (10 or 11years) he can be part of creating the solution. This is very empowering for him, because when he faces problems in his own life, he will have become accustomed to facing them with an attitude of "How can I solve this one?" rather than a feeling of being overwhelmed or defeated.

At first your kids might not understand how to brainstorm. You can give them the idea by starting out the process. Personally, I've found it helpful to suggest totally goofy ideas. "OK, I have an idea. We can throw your sister in the garbage can," as I write it down. This conveys what I mean by brainstorming and also conveys that any idea is acceptable, and won't be judged. This way they can feel free to let their creative imaginations flow. Consider and choose strategies until you find strategies that meet both parties' needs.

5. MAKING AMENDS

Many conflict resolution models don't include a step for making amends. I think it is essential to teach children that making amends is what you do when you make a mistake, and it teaches them how to do that. When one makes a mistake it isn't necessary to walk around forever with a bad label or bad feeling about oneself. By making amends, one can shed the offender label and regain a positive standing in society and a positive view of oneself.

Though it is best if amends are voluntary and come from the child's own initiative, sometimes consequences are in order and they must be mandated by the parent; for example, cleaning up a mess, or replacing something broken. You can say, "Nathan, how might you make amends to your friend?" and let him come up with an idea. Or you can make a suggestion "Something you might do to make it up to your friend would be to help him with his sweeping chore tomorrow." But if damage has been done, then you might mandate, "You'll have to return this stolen gum to the store," or "You'll have to pay for his book that you ruined." You wouldn't want to force her to say "I'm sorry" because that would be asking her to be insincere.

6. FOLLOWING THROUGH

So many adults I know create beautiful and well meaning intentions. They visualize where they want to go and how they want it to be, but so few of them possess the rare skill of being able to manifest their intentions. By following up with your children, making sure they remember to act on their positive intentions, you will help your children to develop integrity and strengthen their will.

These six principles are in common use; I have simply put them into a mnemonic form "How to Feel Nice With All Folks". I figure we need a mnemonic since we parents have to be able to recall the steps in many diverse circumstances – when we are driving and one child just threw the other's lunch out the window, when we are at a fancy restaurant and . . . .

I call this process Refereeing, since this dialogue is often used to help two or more children resolve a conflict between them, but these basic conflict resolution principles can be applied in many different relationships. You can use this acronym to help create effective dialogue between yourself and your spouse, between siblings, between your child and his friends, and even between your child and someone who isn't even there.

HOW TO REFEREE

1. Love each child.
   (This is mandatory. If you feel judgment against a child, you will probably do more harm than good.) Assume the intrinsic goodness of their nature. Look for positive intent.

2. Ask Referee questions (see next page) while at the same time doing the following:
   Remind them about Ground Rules. (It is helpful sometimes to agree upon these in advance. For example; no interrupting, no name calling, no screaming, no running away, etc.)

   —Helpful, but not so essential other stuff—

   Reframe language:
"can't"	to	"You chose not to"
"had to"	to	"You chose to"
"he thinks/wants/feels"	to	"It's your view that he thinks/wants/feels"

Name feelings (i.e. help them talk)
  "It seems to me that you were feeling very frustrated?"

Name and Validate Needs
  "We all want to feel included..."

3. Ask children to mirror.

If you sense that either child is so overwhelmed with emotion and so intensely focused on his own side that he isn't listening to the other person's story, you can ask him to mirror.

Mirroring isn't agreeing.

"Marion, I'd like you to repeat back to Tony what he just said to you."

If she is unable to mirror, there is no need to chastise her; simply ask Tony to say it again for her. This time, knowing she will be asked to repeat it, Marion will be more likely to listen.

HOW TO FEEL NICE WITH ALL FOLKS
CONFLICT RESOLUTION

HOW TO
(Happened)

What happened in your view?
Just say observable actions. This way you will avoid putting in interpretations such as saying what other people felt, thought or were motivated by. Not "When you were being mean" but rather, "when you took my pencils."

FEEL
(Feelings)

"When _____ happened, I felt ___"
Note that felt ___ needs to be an emotion as in "I felt sad." "Felt like" or "felt that" won't work, as in "I felt like you were a jerk."

NICE
(Need)

What were you needing?
I.e., why you took the action you did. What did you want? Identify positive intent. Distinguish needs from the strategies to meet them. Use the attached needs list.

Second person mirrors (What I hear you saying is)
————————Repeat with second person sending————————

WITH
(Way)

Someone articulate both needs.
What strategy can we come up with that will meet both of our needs? The "let's brainstorm" atmosphere is what you are aiming for here. Check whether brainstormed strategies meet all needs, pick one or more strategies.

ALL
(Amends)

Does anyone choose to make amends?
Are there mandatory amends?

FOLKS
(Future)

Shall we check back in in the future?

NEEDS LIST

CONNECTION	HONESTY	MEANING
acceptance	authenticity	awareness
affection	integrity	celebration of life
appreciation	presence	challenge
belonging		clarity
cooperation	PLAY	competence
communication	joy	consciousness
closeness	humor	contribution
community		creativity
companionship	PEACE	discovery
compassion	beauty	efficacy
consideration	communion	effectiveness
consistency	ease	growth
empathy	equality	hope
inclusion	harmony	learning
intimacy	inspiration	mourning
love	order	participation
mutuality		purpose
nurturing	PHYSICAL WELL-	self-expression
respect/self-respect	BEING	stimulation
safety	air	to matter
security	food	understanding
stability	movement/exercise	
support	rest/sleep	AUTONOMY
to know and be known	sexual expression	choice
to see and be seen	safety	freedom
to understand and be understood	shelter	independence
	touch	space
trust	water	spontaneity
warmth		

Exercise Thirty Eight

MOVING FROM I.C.E. TO HOW TO FEEL NICE WITH ALL FOLKS

In the I.C.E. acronym, you are in control – you are taking the role of authority. This provides the stable tricycle which young children need. While you are, of course, considering the child's wishes in your decision making, you aren't asking the child about his inclinations, asking her to intellectualize about her needs, or asking her to make the decision or even be included in the process of making the decision about what is going to happen in the life of the family.

To ask a child to engage in these processes at this young age would be tantamount to asking a 6m old baby to stand up. The baby could manage it but only by unnaturally tensing his thigh muscles. This premature use of the muscles would prevent their proper eventual development. All things in their time! A young child's introspective forces are naturally dormant and best left dormant until they are more mature.

Just as training wheels are used to gradually move a child from a trike to a 12 speed, you will want to gradually move your child into dialoging. Since all children develop differently, this is something you will have to feel your way through.

WITH / WAY

When the child reaches school age, you might want to begin giving him a peek into your decision making process. Instead of just stating choices/consequences you might say the "because" as well. I'm not referring to the ubiquitous "because I said so", but rather the real reason why he has to go to bed, "because otherwise, you'll be too tired tomorrow to enjoy yourself at the beach." You might speak the conflicting needs out loud so your child can begin to understand that your decisions often need to incorporate conflicting needs and desires. "I'd love to let you stay and play here longer, but your sister's lesson is ending soon and she'd be upset if we weren't there to pick her up on time."

FEEL / FEEL

Rather than asking the child to speak her own feelings, as the acronym suggests, you might simply speak the feelings out loud. "It seems you are unhappy about this?" or "I see you are angry about this but your yelling has made me angry as well!" or "You girls are having a great time but it looks like Katie is feeling left out." This way you are acknowledging feelings without prematurely encouraging introspection.

NICE / NEEDS

Needs can be handled in the same way. The idea here is to make a guess at positive intent. Rather than ask the young child to introspect and think logically and deeply about his own inner motivations, just stay on the surface as much as possible, "Were you trying to join in the game because you needed to belong?" "Did you think the umpire made an unfair call and are needing equity?"

You are a mirror for your child. However you see her, she will see herself. If you see her as "bad," she will identify with that. If you can separate her from her behavior, and see her as an intrinsically good person who did a harmful, or unskillful behavior, then she will identify with that.

Seeing her as bad sounds like, "Jill! There you go again bothering your sister! What's wrong with you? Why can't you just leave her alone?"

Separating her from her behavior sounds like, "Jill, when you interrupt your sister while she's playing with her friends, she gets very annoyed at you. Do you wish you had friends over too? Yeah. This is hard for you. How about helping cook dinner? You can cut the mushrooms with your play knife."

An incident that illustrates this principle happened with a group of 11 year old girls. One girl was verbally bullying the class target and the targeted girl began to cry. I spoke with the girl who was bullying alone. "It seems that Millie is very upset by what you said." She crossed her arms, raised her eyebrows and said, "Millie is just sooooo sensitive!" She was trying to turn the blame over to Millie and her oversensitivity. Ignoring her negative meaning of the word "sensitive," I held up a positive picture of her so she could choose to identify with it. "Wow!" I said, "That's kind of you to notice how sensitive your friend is. Good work! Because of this, of course, the girls in your class will have to be extra careful not to hurt her feelings. How might you help the other girls to accomplish this?" To my surprise she took the bait. Her arms uncrossed, her face softened, and she began to fill her need for esteem through this positive leadership rather than through the attention-getting behavior of abusing the target. Admittedly, this is an extreme example, and certainly this small incident didn't affect a long term cure, but this is the sort of support that if done consistently, can move a child towards more constructive behaviors.

FOLKS / FAIR / FUTURE

It goes without saying that you can't expect young children to be conscious enough to follow through on needed behavioral changes by themselves. If you don't do it, it likely won't happen.

The same applies to fairness. You can't expect young children to be responsible to speak up when the resolution decided on by the group is uncomfortable for them. Don't accept tacit approval. Check in with them, "Does this feel OK to you?" I'm not saying that it is necessary for them to like it or approve of it (if you've just stated amends such as 'you'll have to clean this up,' it isn't necessary for them to like it). I'm just saying not to assume that they feel resolved without checking with them. (See the end of the following Case of the Pencils and the Paint.)

Jane Martin

Exercise Thirty Nine

REFEREEING IN ACTION — SOME SAMPLE CASES

The case of Pencils and Paint

Tommy, who is covered with paint, hits Sally over the head with a book.

HOW TO/ FEEL (HAPPENED / FEELINGS)

Sally, what just happened here in your view?

Sally: He hit me!

Tommy: Well she threw paint on me for no reason!

Tommy could you please refrain from interrupting Sally until she is done? She will give you the same courtesy in just a minute. Sally, go ahead.

Sally: He took my pencils off my desk. He takes my stuff all the time....

And then? (sometimes you gotta pump out the part of the story she'd rather forget)

Sally: And then I threw paint on him and then he hit me! I'm telling my mother!

So when you saw him taking the pencils, you felt angry?

Sally: Yeah

Tommy, what happened in your view?

Tommy: She is just a big fat liar, those ...

Tommy, it isn't really helpful to call Sally names. You can just tell us what happened.

Tommy: Those are my pencils! They have my name on the back. I was just taking them and then for no reason at all, she just threw paint on me!

And then?

Tommy: Then I hit her.

So when she threw paint on you, you felt really really angry?

Tommy: Nods and crosses arms.

FEELING PART STILL, BUT HELPING THEM MIRROR

So Sally, you believed that when Tommy was taking the pencils that he was borrowing them from you without asking, right? But now that you heard Tommy's point of view, what do you think?

Sally: Oh, they are his. Sorry.

Tommy, you mentioned that you believed that Sally had no reason to throw paint on you. Now that you hear her view, can you think of what her reason was to do that?

Tommy: Because she thought they were her pencils.

NICE / WITH (NEED / WAY)

Sally, it seems that you don't like it when Tommy takes your stuff without asking. What could you have done today to get that need met without hurting Tommy?

Sally: I could have told him, "Give it back you big jerk!"

Tommy, would that way have been good for you, or do you have another suggestion?

Tom: She could just say, "Those are my pencils and then I'd say no they're mine - see my name?"

Does that sound OK Sally?

Sally: Yeah

ALL (AMENDS)

Sally, how can you make amends to Tommy?

Sally: I can wash out his shirt.

Tommy: OK

WITH (WAY)

Tommy, when Sally threw paint on you, you felt really mad, right? What else could you have done to let Sally know this, besides hit?

Tommy: I could say, "What's your problem girl?"

And how can you make amends to her?

Tommy: OK! OK! I won't hit her.

Yes, that's great, but what can you do to make amends to Sally now?

Tommy: Sorry I hit you Sally.

FOLKS (FAIR)

So, are we OK here?

Sally: But he does always take my stuff.

Tommy, Sally is requesting that you ask her before using her stuff, is that OK with you?

Tommy: Yeah, OK.

Exercise Forty

The case of the Little Clique

You are in a restaurant with 7 girls. A place is appropriated for all 7 girls to sit for lunch. You see two girls go make a separate spot for "the 5 of us." The 2 other girls look on with forlorn faces.

HOW TO/FEEL (WHAT HAPPENED / FEELINGS)

Yo! Little Dudettes! Come over here for a sec. I see you are making a separate spot over there. What's going on?

Cutey Kid: Well, we just want to sit together, that's all.

That's great to sit with your friends. I'm thinking though, that maybe the other two girls might feel a bit left out. What do you think?

CK : I don't know. They didn't *say* that. We aren't trying to exclude them, we just like to sit together with just us, that's all.

Well, I'm big now, but I still remember being 10, and I might feel left out if I were them. Even if they felt left out, they might not say it.

CK: I guess

WITH (WAY)

What can you do to make sure that you don't accidentally hurt your friends' feelings?

CK: We can ask them if they want to sit with us.

That sounds great! You're the kind of friend I would want to have!

(Note there is no amends, because the prevention *is* the amends)

Jane Martin

Exercise Forty One

The Case of the Timid Pusher

You see a little girl sitting mournfully by herself at recess. You sit next to her to chat. She tells you that she wishes she could play with the girls who are making up a skit, but they won't let her.

Have you asked to be in the skit?

Timid Pusher: Yes, but they said I couldn't.

Would you like me to help you talk with them?

TP: (makes some slight sign of affirmation) but they'll just say no...

HOW TO / FEEL (WHAT'S GOING ON / FEELINGS)

Hey guys, I'd like to talk with you all for a second. TP here, says there's some problem with her being in the skit? Can you tell me what that problem might be?

Skit Girl: We just don't have any room left in the skit, that's all.

Hmmm, I see, that's a difficult problem to solve. But I think TP might be feeling sort of left out. I'm sure you wouldn't want the other girls to leave you out right?! That just doesn't feel good to anyone! Is there a way you might work out a part for TP?

SG: We don't *want* her to be in it!

Oh! I see! Can you tell us the reason for that?

SG: Not really. We just don't.

SG, if there is some problem you are having with your friend, it is important to speak to her about it. You are telling her that you are having a problem with her by excluding her, but that doesn't help the situation out, since she still doesn't know what the problem is. If you can communicate with her, then maybe you can work the problem out in a way that won't make her feel bad. (Here you are not accepting their method, which is the norm now, to not speak out their problems for fear of hurting the other person's feelings)

SG: Well, she makes *us* feel bad!

Can you tell her, when you do such and such, we feel such and such?

SG: When you push our arms, we feel really annoyed.

TP, SG is saying that sometimes you push her arm, and that she doesn't like that. Do you know what she is talking about?

TP: Yes, I guess so

So, she is requesting that you not do that. What is it that you are needing when you do that?

TP: I just want them to listen to me.

TP wants to be listened to, and some of these girls don't want to have their arms pushed. That's our pickle. What great ideas can you guys come up with to solve this? etc.

Exercise Forty Two

The case of the Overflowing Mouth

You get a call saying that your child was rude to his music teacher.

FEEL (WHAT HAPPENED / FEELINGS)

Dude, park yourself over here, will ya? No, no, next to me so I can hug you. (cuddling) (with humor) Rumor has it that some not so nice language has been leaking out of your mouth in music class! Can you tell me what's going on?

Overflowing Mouth: Well, ummm, (fidget fidget, looking over there) It's her fault!

Right now, I don't even know what went on, can you fill me in?

OM: Today, class was so stupid and boring and so Barney and I were throwing our pencils to each other, and then she yelled at me, and so I told her to go shove it.

So, you were feeling bored in class, and tried to have some fun with Barney and then when the teacher yelled at you, you felt angry?

(Now, to do it backward, you have to pretend the teacher is there and guess the teacher's feelings)

I'm just wondering, how do you think the teacher felt when she was trying to do her job and teach music and she saw you chucking pencils?

OM: (with a startled look, like, but I never thought of the teacher as a human being before!) I don't know, I guess she didn't like it.

NICE / WITH (NEED / WAY)

I'd guess probably not. She probably didn't have to bellow at you, I agree. You'd probably have preferred if she would have spoken to you respectfully and expressed that she didn't like your pencil chucking, right?

OM: Yeah.

But that's what she did do. So, what were your choices? You were bored - what could you have done that wouldn't have bothered your teacher or your friends?

OM: I could do clay in my desk. Or I could tell her that I was bored. Or I could tell my main teacher that I hate music and am bored. Or I could just sit there and be bored. Or I could sing myself a song. Or I could invent a Nintendo game in my head. Or I could try to be the best at what she was teaching. Or I could.....

You have an incredible capacity for problem solving! Now let's see if you can apply that to your other choice - you felt angry when she yelled, what else could you have done besides say, "Shove it" that wouldn't have upset your teacher?

OM: I could say what you said before, that I would prefer that she just speak to me respectfully and say that she didn't like my pencil chucking because it was making her feel bad. I could tell her that I feel mad when she yells at me.

ALL (AMENDS)

I think those are all great ideas. Your teacher seems to be still very angry with you since she had your main teacher call me. What do you think you can do to resolve this problem?

OM: I can tell her all that stuff I just said!

Yes, you could. And maybe even throw in a little apology for saying "shove it," while you're at it. I'll bet she'd appreciate that.

OM: OK, I'll do it tomorrow at school.

Cool.

Exercise Forty Three

Some cases for you to practice with

1. It's a birthday party and 15 girls are setting up their sleeping bags with their heads facing into a circle. Two girls (who are best friends and tend to pull away from the group) decide to put their feet into the center. Other girls object.

2. You: Who's going to clean up this mess? Big Sister (sneering): I guess I have to since there's no way *she's* going to help. Little sister kicks big sister's chair.

3. Your son comes in from a ball game, looks on the table and sees there is no dessert left for him. He stomps out and slams his door.

4. Rough and tumble boy, in play, grabs prissy little girl to steal her and put her in the dungeon. She begins to cry and runs to you, expecting you to punish him.

5. Your daughter comes home upset because her friend was mean to another girl in the class.

6. You overhear this: Skate Dude: I have the best skateboard ever made in the universe. Your skateboard sucks.
    Self Righteous Dude: You think you are so great. It's really mean of you to say this stuff.
    Skate Dude kicks Self Righteous Dude's skateboard into the street.

7. You witness two boys carrying off a girl and throwing her in the dungeon pretty roughly. She screeches at them and throws grass at them. You check out her face and she's smiling brightly.

8. Your little one is very tired and hungry. You ask her to pour some milk in the recipe you are making. She accidentally drops the milk. She throws a huge fit, chucking the milk carton across the room.

9. Your little 10 year old prodigy plays his violin at 8 am on a weekend and wakes up your teenager. Your teenager bodily picks up the 10 year old and removes him from the house, locking the door.

10. Big Sister: That's not fair! She woke me up this morning, and she did it on purpose, so she should have to clean the kitchen for me for a year!

Exercise Forty Four

INNER MAGIC

"There is no sin, save the accusation of sin."
—William Blake

Have you ever wondered how a dog can sense whether a stranger is friend or foe? They are never fooled by a phony show of kindness, nor by the most macho motorcycle gang style of dress and demeanor. They seem to be able to sense inside the person. I hope it isn't rude to say that kids are a bit like dogs (at least in this respect).

Sometimes people come back to me and say, "I tried your system but my child is still a little brat. Your system doesn't work." What needs to change isn't something in the system, in the words or in the actions this mother uses. What needs to change is something deep inside her. And these are the glasses through which she views her child. Because despite what she says or does, her child can sense this pair of glasses, just as a dog can sense the inner nature of a stranger.

My daughter, Lily, is currently in a production of Arthur Miller's The Crucible, which is about the Salem Witch Trials. I understand that historians have discovered that in the year of these trials, a fungus grew on the Salem rye crop. This fungus, called ergot, was psychotropic, meaning it would cause hallucinations when eaten.

When faced with community members who were hallucinating and behaving in ways that were beyond their understanding, the church elders of Salem simply labeled the behavior as Satanic, and judged the people, condemning them as witches. They solved this community problem by cleansing the so-called witches from their midst - punishing them by hanging or burning them.

So I'm looking at this situation, this play, as highlighting the tendency of people, when faced with something they can't understand, to judge and label it. This judging, this separating the phenomenon from one's self, makes people feel safer.

When our children behave in ways that upset us and we become fearful because we're not able to control or even to comprehend their behavior - that is the time to be aware of this human tendency to judge, punish, and blame. It's like putting on a pair of glasses that overlay the label "bad" on top of the child.

If you find yourself (or more accurately, I should say "when you find yourself," because we almost all do it at some point) in this position, this is the opportunity for you to try a new way. I call it "glasses switching."

If you hear words coming out of your mouth (gosh, where do these words come from anyway?) calling your child "a brat," "a little devil," "bad," "naughty," "rotten," "lazy," or any other negative label, let it be a clue for you to take a moment to perform the following exercise:

GLASSES SWITCHING EXERCISE

1. Close your eyes.
2. Take 10 very full breaths, filling your belly, your chest and letting it go. (Don't skip this step as there is a physiological reason for it.)
3. Imagine your child before you, enacting the most recent unacceptable and unexplainable behavior. Get a good clear picture, include sound and surroundings if you can.
4. Envision her body coming inside of your body.
5. Now she is inside of you. You can even let your body take on her posture and facial expression and movements, so that you can really feel how it is to be her.
6. Notice the body sensations you have - is there a sense of anger, or maybe also sadness, embarrassment, confusion, or fear?

List some emotions that you sense here:

_____

7. Pretending that you are her in that situation, let yourself speak for her and say, "I'm wanting _____."

8. Then say, "I'm wanting _____ because I'm needing

_____."

Let yourself speak for her until you understand her deep human motivation for her actions.

Write them here:

_____

9. Remember back to a time when you, yourself, had that same need. Possibly you were more adept at filling it. Possibly you had the skill to fill your need without bothering other people.

But right now that isn't what is important. What is important is the validation of the right of this child to have, and to try to fill, this need.

A time I experienced that need was _____

_____

10. This is the release of judgment. When you succeed, you will notice that something inside of you unclenches. You will feel your defenses and your anger, just drop away. You will automatically feel a compassion for the child and a desire to truly help her. It is as if you have removed your glasses with the negative label on them, and put on new glasses of acceptance.

11. To truly help her, you can teach her an alternative way to fulfill her need. A way that won't hurt other people, her future self, or her environment. In order to help her to find this new way, you must be aware of her true need. This exercise helps you to become aware of what is truly going on inside your child.

I would like my child to fill her need by _____

_____

When this is your inner state, when you are wearing the glasses of acceptance, then you can even mess up the system entirely, and still truly help your child. And when your inner state is clenched, wearing the glasses of judgment, and viewing the child as bad, you can perform every system in the world to a T, and never achieve satisfactory results.

If you see your child as "bad," she will identify with that and she will become it. But when you can see the deep core goodness of your child, and speak to it, this enables your child to identify and to become it as well. This is the inner magic that really makes any discipline system work.

Exercise Forty Five

END OF DAY REVIEW WITH KIDS

Just as you can elevate your own life using the contemplative review of the End of Day Review exercise, you can also elevate your child's life. Adding 15 minutes, at bedtime, to your daily routine, will provide a safe space for your child to process and learn from the events of his day. Sitting on a rocking chair or cuddling in the child's bed while holding him close will help him to relax and feel safe.

Basically, just like with your own End of Day Review, you would tell the story of the child's day:

"First you woke up, then you ate oatmeal and were giggling about the baby making such a mess, then you kicked the dog, then…..:"

Use a matter of fact, nonjudgmental tone. Connect with child on the level of humor or empathy.

At key points that hold an emotional charge, you may choose to empathize with the emotion:

"Then you kicked the dog….. Gee it seems like you were upset then?"

Don't worry about guessing an incorrect emotion; the child will correct you, "No I was mad at her because she ate my sock."

Feel free to just sit with the emotion, and not try to fix it. Just mirror it. "Oh, so you were feeling really mad because Spot ate your sock…… I see….."

This may seem not helpful at all, but it is extremely healing for a child to be seen and deeply understood

When the above is done, if it seems appropriate, (i.e. the child seems ready) you can move the conversation into Brainstorming or teaching mode. For children approximately 6 yrs old and under "Hmmmm, kicking the dog isn't ok. It hurts her. When you are mad you can come ask for my help instead."

For children 7 and up "Hmmmm, kicking the dog isn't ok. It hurts her. What might you have done instead?"

Brainstorm options with the child.

Then go over the options and say, "And what might be the consequences of *that* option, do you think?"

Then the child will be able to choose an option with your guidance.

If this brainstorm part doesn't happen, that is totally ok. This is icing on the cake.

The cake is that you are giving your child deep attention. You are giving him a space to work through his conflicts. You are giving him a way to learn new behaviors to meet his needs, so that he can give up behaviors that are not working or are hurting others. You are giving him a way to express his needs in words rather than in negative actions. You are cuddling, giving him the physical nurturing touch and quiet space that all humans need. Even if you don't 'fix' everything, you are demonstrating that you care. That is *huge*.

This is where your child can open up, and feel safe from punishment or blame, knowing she will receive acceptance for her 'faults' and 'mistakes.' She can tell you what is truly going on with her. Then she is not alone in the world.

It is a beautiful gift to give a child. It is especially beautiful if he knows that he can count on these 15-20 minutes of End of Day Review time every night. Just like he can count on dinner being there, he can count on this safe loving space. Then, during the day, when tough things happen, he can say to himself, "At End of Day Review with dad tonight, I can figure this out." It will be a source of strength to him every day.

I ask my clients to do this exercise with their children. I don't believe that my role as a therapist is to directly 'heal' the child. I believe my role is to empower the parents to continually heal the child. This exercise is really teaching you to be something of a therapist for your child. My clients often will discover the source of their child's problems during this time. Sometimes our children have some major misunderstandings about life and we don't even realize it. Discovering these beliefs gives you the opportunity to heal the problem.

Some examples of End of Day Review helping parents to heal their children: 'She was under the impression that because we adopted her, we might adopt another child and give her away! Where did she get this idea? No wonder she has been afraid to leave her mother to go to kindergarten." or "When I got to the part of the day where he made a mistake, he told me he didn't want to do End of Day Review anymore. I realized then that I shame him about making mistakes. No wonder he is so anxious all the time. I am expecting him to be perfect." "Even though she is 13 years old, my daughter and I still do End of Day Review every few days when we cuddle. During it she told me that her boyfriend has been pressuring her to have sex. I had no idea this was going on. She still seems so young to me. And I'm sure she wouldn't have told me this during the day when she is trying to act so grown up and sophisticated.

Exercise Forty Six

THE TEEN YEARS – THE BIOLOGICAL DRIVE
TOWARD AUTONOMY

"Authority as an educational principle no longer applies with the onset of puberty. The young person wishes to acknowledge older people as leaders through friendship. A great deal of misery of family life is caused by parents retaining their authoritarian attitude when their children have reached puberty and they do not succeed in guiding them in friendship. Quite rightly the child now experiences authority as an insult to his personality."
—*Bernard Lievegoed, Phases of Childhood*

Now your child has reached puberty. You are beginning to feel the stirrings of adolescent rebellion. Suddenly in the eyes of your child, you are no longer the all knowing, wonderful human being you once were. In fact, you seem to get stupider every day. "*Oh Gaaawd Mom!*" she says, rolling her eyes.

I would like to invite you to view this time in the same way you viewed the time when your child was one year old and just learning to walk. At both times a biological urge is emerging. Both urges are toward growth and health. Where the one year old's urge is to learn to walk, the teen urge is to learn to become autonomous. The teen senses that in just a few short years, he will have to be able to be out in the world on his own – without you. And now is the time to prepare for that. That preparation doesn't happen all in one day either; just like any growth process, it requires time and patience. He must learn to make good decisions. And he will learn best by doing it. Sometimes skillfully, and sometimes not.

You will remember from the earlier discussion about Inner Freedom that making good decisions requires the four skills. It means that your child must be able to use his Inner Adult to consider the wishes of his Inner Child without being compelled by them, and consider the admonitions of his Inner Parent without being constrained by them.

My husband worked at a college counseling center. So many kids would come in feeling lost and out of control. Their parents kept them on a tricycle throughout their teens, and they never learned to balance their bikes. They were told what to do and their choice was to obey their parents or be punished. They never had to make decisions based on the circumstances at hand. To weigh the pros and cons. To consider their own needs conjointly with those of other people. To choose between what they felt like doing now, and what would benefit them in the long run. To develop their own values, to learn to think deeply into what it means to be "right" or "wrong." They never had to do this, because their parents kept on doing it for them. They never learned how to make decisions.

Then, all at once, they went off to college and their lives were a mess. They had to make their own decisions, but they had never learned to do this skill well. They did what they felt like doing, without regard for the consequences. Their parents had always been the ones to consider the consequences, and the kids' job was just to butt up against the parents in an effort to do what they wanted. But now, no one was stopping them from doing what they wanted. And the consequences of doing whatever they felt like doing were manifesting in their lives! Mayhem!

Imagine what would happen if you didn't let the one year old try to balance herself. Imagine how she would react if you continually held on to her shoulders as she was trying to learn to walk? Rather than supporting her in her efforts toward growth, you'd be thwarting her. Surely, she would fight you! She would rebel with all her might! If you saw this happening to another parent, and you heard that parent saying, "Oh, she is such a bad kid. Always fighting us!" what would you say?" Might you suggest that the parent try to support the child in her efforts to walk? Might you make note of the fact that this would require some bravery on the part of the parent to let go, and to accept that she might fall now and then? Might you also note that this wouldn't mean to *totally* let go, to leave the room and ignore her. Of course, if she toddled too close to the staircase, the parent must take action to protect her.

Now imagine your teenager. He is feeling a biological urge to be independent in the world. If you can support this growth *you do not have to fight with your teen!* Most parents of teenagers think I'm a bit off my rocker when I say this. Their experience is that life with their teenager is just one big long fight. But it is my strong belief that the cause of the constant struggles between parent and teen lies much more with the parent than with the teen. If their child is butting up against them, fighting them, because the parents aren't supporting their natural drive towards autonomy, I feel glad! It's the kids who accept the overcontrol, who retreat and become wimpy and lifeless that I worry about. These are not "good" kids; these are kids who have given up. Again I must stress – if you respect the child's natural growth towards taking responsibility for her own life, there is no reason your child's teenage years can't be free (or relatively free) of parent/child conflicts. Your relationship with them can be pleasant and full of love.

So the first point is – it is natural for your teenager to begin to try to make his own decisions in life. If you interfere with this natural process, you will end up in conflict. If you support the child in his efforts to learn and grow, there is no need for fighting.

WHAT TO DO?

Here's what I suggest, and I will elaborate in the following exercises:

1. GRADUALLY, HAND OVER THE REINS OF YOUR CHILD'S LIFE

A. Share your plan with your teen.

B. Move from Parent – Child interactions, to Adult – Adult interactions.

C. Watch your words.

D. Let him decide, even if it's a "mistake."

2. WATCH OVER HIM

A. If he is about to irreparably hurt himself, the environment, or others – take back the reins.

B. Guide his decision making; put in your two cents.

C. If mistakes are made, support him in learning from the mistake- If he makes a mistake in dealing with natural law, point it out. If he makes a mistake and hurts another person, point out how that person might feel. If he makes a mistake and hurts you, tell him how you feel; be human.

If he is violating you, don't be a doormat, decide what you will do.

3. HAVE PATIENCE DURING THE TRANSITION

Exercise Forty Seven

HANDING OVER THE REINS OF YOUR CHILD'S LIFE

When your child was young, it was appropriate for you to face her, with your back to the world, providing a barrier, a protection for her, so she could feel safe and taken care of. If you didn't do this, she wouldn't have the skills to deal with the world, and she would get hurt.

But now that your goal is to help your teen learn to deal with the world, you will need to step aside and let her face the world. How else will she learn? Don't won't walk away from her; just stand next to her. You and she, together, facing the world. You are by her side, with support and advice.

Teens whose parents continue to stand facing them, must try to face the difficulties of the world AND the difficulties of their parents at the same time. With no support! They don't usually fare well.

Your job here is to move from authority to guidance.

SHARE YOUR PLAN WITH YOUR TEEN

How does this translate to real life? What am I suggesting you do? I am suggesting that you begin to allow your child to make some decisions about her own life. If this is unusual for you, it might be helpful to consciously let your child know what you are going to be doing:

"Alice, from now on, it will be your decision what you do when you get home from school. I think you can manage your time by yourself. At first, we can talk in the car on the way home from school about what you have to do that day, and I can help you to decide when to do what. But as soon as you feel comfortable deciding without me, that will be fine. It may happen that you make some mistakes now and then, and maybe run out of time to do your homework or something, but that's OK, just come to me and we'll work out how to deal with it. I'm sure you will do your best."

What I am suggesting is that step by step, you begin to do the same thing with the rest of her life, until she is responsible for her entire life, like any adult. Each child will need to go at a different speed, of course. You can judge for yourself – as soon as she is handling one area of life reasonably well, add on another. By the time she is 16 or 17, you will have a competent young adult in your house, who asks you for your help only as she needs it.

FROM PARENT–CHILD TO ADULT-ADULT INTERACTIONS

If you do not initiate the young people,
they will burn the village down to feel the heat.
— African Proverb

In many cultures there is a ceremony, an initiation into the adult society or tribe, which occurs around puberty. The Confirmation or the Bar/Bat Mitzvah are examples. These events signify the full acceptance of the child into the adult community.

An anthropological study found that 94% of cultures, throughout time around the world, have some kind of socially sanctioned method of inducing an altered state of consciousness for emotional healing and spiritual growth. Usually these methods are incorporated into a rite of passage. A rite of passage is a ceremony or process that supports the move from one stage of life to the next.

When our children are 11 or 12 years old, the prefrontal cortex of their brain begins to proliferate. More brain matter grows. And this biological addition brings with it, new capacities. Just as our one year olds, as they become ready to walk, begin to experience a biological drive to walk, our teenagers also begin to experience a biological drive to use these new prefrontal cortex capacities.

One of these capacities is to make conscious decisions, i.e. holding both sides of an issue in mind at once. This is why it is so important for parents of teens to begin to move from authority to guidance. Other capacities that are arising in the teen years are a stronger identity, or sense of self, or what we might call 'ego.'

Another PFC capacity, that tends to be overlooked by our society, is the capacity for transcendence. Transcendence means to have an altered state experience; to experience something beyond the material realm.

Candace Pert, Chief of Brain Biochemistry at the National Institutes of Health, made the connection between transcendence and the prefrontal cortex, ""In long term meditators, the frontal cortex starts to light up and shows itself to be very active. If there's a part of the brain that has God in it, the frontal cortex is the way I think about it. That's not very scientific!"

So this transcendent capacity arises with the proliferation of the frontal lobes (my experience is that it is at age 14 that this really takes hold) and the teen also experiences a strong biological drive towards these experiences. If we provide no socially sanctioned channel, they will go for these experiences in their own ways, and often these ways are quite dangerous. This line of thinking is not well known in our culture, so I am listing many quotes here to illustrate this idea.

These studies confirm that when youth lack a rite of passage experience, there are extraordinary consequences related to such problem behaviors as violence, substance use, gangs, bullying, and delinquency. Citations in professional literature and popular media ascribe risk-taking behavior of youth (Lewis and Lewis 1984; Merten 2005) as their attempts to create

rites of passage for themselves. Rites of passage during adolescence, Scott D. Scheer*
Stephen M. Gavazzi
The Ohio State University
David G. Blumenkrantz Center for the Advancement of Youth, Family, and Community Services, Inc.

One reason for the great demand for psychiatric services for adolescents today may be the absence of socially sanctioned rites of passage. Throughout human history these rites have served humanity well. The desire for some rites and rituals at puberty as well as at the end of the teen years is natural, even today. Young people seem to want the real thing, an authentic initiation. There is truly a 'hunger for initiation.'
Louise Carus Mahdi

In modern culture, our Rites of Passage are often missing or minimized in importance. We seem to have lost many of our communal and sanctioned ways of taking risks and acknowledging the transition from childhood to adulthood.

Daniel Siegel, M.D., Brainstorm: The power and purpose of the teenage brain.

Most spiritual life calls for times of sudden radical transformation brought about by powerful initiation and rites of passage. For modern young men and women this is a desperate need. If nothing is offered in the way of initiation to prove one's entry into the world of men and women, it will be done unguided in the road or the street with cars at high speed, with drugs, with weapons.

155

Jane Martin

Jack Kornfield, Ph.D., Psychologist and Buddhist teacher

*The well known anthropologist, Margaret Meade, believed that
the fact that modern society has lost sanctioned rites of passage is a critical
contributing factor to the increase of various forms of social pathology.*
-Christina Grof

This is why rites of passages are so crucial to our teens and why it is so important to re-introduce them into our culture. Yes, there are Bar Mitzvah's and Confirmations, but these tend to be more of a commemoration of the move from childhood to adulthood, rather than the transformative process to create the inner maturation itself. Some rite of passage programs try to recreate indigenous ceremonies, and they are wonderful retreats for teens, but they tend to lack the altered state experience which is so core to the transformation.

The news is full of reports of our young adults going through an 'extended adolescence.' There is much consternation about the inability of our young adults to take up responsibility for their lives. I contend that a rite of passage would help with this.

For a modern day rite of passage program for teens, with altered state processes, see www.ReTribe.org

Now is the time to begin treating the child more like an adult, so that he can begin to learn to act like one. Talking to your child from your adult to his adult should sound similar to the way you would speak to a friend in your home. How does this sound?

Parent to Child:

"Young man, you may not watch TV until your homework is done."

Adult to Adult:

"Jim, I see you are watching TV. You remembered to do your homework, right?"

Take a moment to read the first example and notice how you would *feel,* how you would be inclined to react if you were Jim. Can you notice the feeling of being against your parent? Do you feel the assumption of the parent that you are trying to be "bad," and that if she didn't stop you, you would blow off your homework?

Now read the second example. Notice how much more like an adult it makes you feel. Notice the expectation of the parent that you did remember your homework. And notice how it would feel if you had forgotten. You could simply say "Gosh, I forgot. Thanks for reminding me," with no guilt and no shame – and then you could just go ahead and do it. You might even think to yourself how you might remember by yourself tomorrow.

WATCH YOUR WORDS

The switch is hard. You are changing a longstanding habit. Try watching your words. Particularly notice the words "should/shouldn't," "you better," "must," "allowed," "can/can't," "may/may not," "do as I say," etc. At the end of each day, think back over your conversations and track your progress towards an adult to adult relationship.

Remember, this is a gradual change. A young teen often reverts back to his childlike "needy" nature, especially in times of stress, and that is the time for you to be the parent and comfort and take care of him. He still sometimes needs you to be his parent.

TRULY LET HIM DECIDE

VEERING TO THE RIGHT VS. RUNNING OFF THE ROAD

Many parents feel quite afraid to hand over the reins of their child's life. "What if he makes wrong decisions?" Occasionally, your child is about to make a decision that might irreparably harm himself or others. This is like running off the road. Here it is appropriate to take back the reins and assert your authority. But this kind of situation is very rare. Most of the time when you feel compelled to take back the reins it is because he is making a choice that you wouldn't make. This is like veering to the right. And it could well be that he has every intention of veering back to the left in plenty of time to avoid an accident. But if you take back the reins every time he decides something you don't agree with, then you haven't really given him the reins at all. If you give the child the right to make a decision, you must allow "wrong" decisions. So maybe he decides to stay up late one night and he is very tired the next day. This kind of natural consequence is just what he may need to wake him up to the unyielding discipline the world dispenses. And next time he will probably decide differently. He made a mistake. He learned from it. This is fine.

LETTING HIM STAY IN THE MIDDLE HIMSELF

Sometimes in workshops when we talk about teens, people will ask, "Oh, when they are teens you go more towards the Mayhem side?" I can see why they would ask that, because there is the element of loosening control. But the idea is still to stay in the middle. There is still the ideal of balancing the needs of self with the needs of others. But with teens, you are trying to let them balance themselves. Just like when they are learning to ride a bike, at some point, you have to let go of the bike and let them learn to balance themselves. If you find that they begin making decisions that go too far towards the mayhem end, and end up hurting themselves or others, you can simply point it out to them or if necessary retake control of the bike for a bit. Or sometimes, you will find that they go too far towards the Boot Camp end, and you will be there to encourage them to honor their own needs too.

Exercise Forty Eight

WATCH OVER HIM

TAKE BACK THE REINS – DAMAGE CONTROL

I want to be clear that I am in no way advocating that you hand over the reins all at once. To expect your child to be fine on her own, making all her own decisions, all of a sudden, just because she happened to turn 13 is unrealistic. I'm saying to hand her the reins of her life, but I'm not saying to jump off the carriage. You can let her hold the reins, while at the same time, your hands are outside of hers, you are making commentary the whole time "Watch out for that tree!" and you are ready to grab the reins if you feel that she is about to run off the road. By run off the road I mean, to irreparably harm herself, her environment or other people.

GUIDING HIM DOESN'T MEAN YOU CAN'T PUT IN YOUR TWO CENTS

Your job is to guide your teen in making decisions. Guiding doesn't mean making decisions for them. They can't learn to do it, if you are doing it. But neither does it mean that you shouldn't state your opinion.

Try asking questions designed to get them thinking about their options. Then ask them more questions designed to get them to think through the options and consider the pros and cons of each.

"Mom, the play director called a rehearsal from 6:00 today, and the performance is tonight. I have to meet with the group of kids I'm doing my physics project with from 3 to 5:00. That only leaves me 1 hour to get dressed and eat dinner, and no time to do my homework! If I go to school tomorrow without my math done, I'll fail the test and get 50 points off for not doing my homework."

"Wow. What a pickle! What can you do?"

"Well I can stay up all night, or I can just get a bad grade this marking period in math, or maybe I can just go in late to school tomorrow."

"What about attendance? Do you have too many absences?"
"No, I only have 3 and you can have 12."

"What would happen if you stayed up late?"

"I don't think it's a good idea because I have 4 more performances and I'm not feeling very well. I'm getting a cold."

"So what do you think is the best option then?"

"I don't know what to do!"

"Well, personally, I don't think it's so bad to take off from school as long as you aren't missing anything important."

Sometimes you will find that your teen is amazingly empty-headed when you ask her about options, or about consequences. That blank look on her face when you say "and what might the consequences of *that* option be?" will clue you in to the importance of going over this process with her many times. So often parents assume that their teen is just naturally able to do this, and when she makes an unwise decision, they judge her as being "bad." What may seem obvious to us is new territory for them. Think of decision making as a skill that requires practice like any other skill. It takes repetition to develop the decision making muscles.

FROM RUBBING IT IN TO POINTING OUT REALITY

We all make mistakes. So expect your teen to do the same. In fact, expect your teen to make mistakes a bit more often than you do. After all, he hasn't learned all the life lessons that you have. He isn't as aware of natural law, or in other words, how the world works.

I have found that it isn't automatic for someone to learn from his mistakes. Often there is such a focus on the mistake itself, the repercussions, the making of amends etc., that the lesson itself just goes by unnoticed. Pulling out the lesson is a wonderful habit that you can help your teen cultivate. How? Simply point out reality.

Rather than:
"Andrew, you said you were just going for a bike ride and you'd be back before lunch. That was 4 hours ago. When you say you are going to do something I expect you to do it. Can't I trust you with anything? It's mistake after mistake with you! Do I have to put you on a leash?"

Try:
"My God, Andrew! You've been gone for hours. We've been so worried! I thought you guys were just going to ride your bikes?"

"We did. But we wanted to ride somewhere so we went to Lambertville. We called a store there to get directions. But we didn't think it would take so long! It didn't seem long when you drove us there."

"Oh I see what happened. So I guess it wasn't such a good idea to bite off so much without knowing whether you could chew it."

"Yeah, next time I won't just get directions, I'll ask how many miles it is too!"

Rather than:
"Marcia, no wonder you forgot your homework – you are so tired. I *told* you to go to bed earlier last night, but did you listen to me? Nooooooo!"

Try:
"Wow. That's a bummer that you forgot your homework. You do seem rather tired to me, maybe that's why? When I don't go to bed on time, I often forget things the next day too."

If your teen is trying to deal with your anger, your blame, and the insinuation that he is trying to be bad, he won't have the psychic energy to think constructively into the future about how he can improve his life skills.

POINT OUT HOW THE OTHER PERSON MIGHT FEEL

Sometimes it may not be obvious to your teen that she made a mistake at all. She might not notice the effects of her actions, especially when the result of her mistake hurt someone else. In such cases, point out how the other person might feel:

Rather than:
"Melinda, I can't believe you just talked about your party right in front of Trish! You know you aren't inviting her. That is so rude. Why would you do such a thing?"

Try:
"Melinda. I noticed you were just talking about the party with Debbie, and Trish was standing right there. I'm thinking she might have hurt feelings right now."

If you were Melinda hearing the first admonishment, your focus would be on the doubt about your own intrinsic kindness. Are you good or are you bad?

If you were Melinda hearing the second, your focus would be on what you can do for Trish. Your intrinsic goodness is assumed.

EXPRESS YOUR HUMANITY – BECOME A PERSON

Sometimes parents translate my suggestion to give the child the reins of his life, into a picture of the child taking the reins of *their* life! "If I let my son do as he wants, he'll take complete advantage of me!" If this thought sounds familiar to you, then I strongly suggest that you make some effort to improve your own relationship skills. Possibly you need to learn to be assertive without being aggressive?

Your child is learning to live in society, and part of living in society is to be able to balance his own needs with those of others. Since this is a new skill, he might accidentally go too far, expressing his needs without regard to you. When this occurs, let him know! This is how he will learn what is too far and what is not too far. The trick is to speak to him in the same way you would speak to another adult living in your house. Convey how it is for *you*. Let him know how *you* feel as a person. This will awaken him to the effects his actions have on other people. This way he can control his actions because of how it will affect someone, rather than because of your controlling him. He needs a chance to practice balancing self and other in relationship.

Rather than:
"Michael! Your clothes are all over the living room again! You act like a slob! If I can't even trust you to clean your clothes up, how am I going to trust you with the car?"

Try:
"Michael, it's a problem for me when you leave your clothes in the living room. I only schedule myself 15 minutes to tidy the house each morning before my clients come over, and I don't want to have to pick up your clothes. What can we do about this?"

Rather than:
"Young lady, that kind of speech will not be tolerated in this house."

Try:
"Katie, when I hear the kind of vulgar language you just used, I feel very uncomfortable. If you choose to speak that way, I'd appreciate it if you'd confine it to your room. It's important to me to be able to be in my own house without being subjected to speech that upsets me."

Rather than:
"Tim, your curfew is 11:30. You know that. You weren't home in time last night so you won't use the car today."

Try:

"Tim, when you weren't home by 12:30 last night, and I hadn't heard from you, I felt really worried. I love you so much and I just couldn't sleep not knowing that you were safe."

WHAT IF HE WON'T BE RESPONSIBLE?
DON'T BE A DOORMAT

For example, what if he doesn't do his chores? What should you do?

First of all, you are highly limited in what you can *make* him do. When he was 3 years old and had a tiny little body, you could just pick him up, and force the situation. But no more! Not with your 5'11" 15 year old son! What can you truly force him to do?

But the reverse is also true. You *can* decide what *you* will do. Or not do.

"Jake, I see your chore isn't done."

"I don't feel like doing it."

"Oh I see. Well we all pitch in as part of this family. We do our responsibilities whether we feel like it or not. What if I don't feel like making you dinner tonight, or I don't feel like driving you to Mary's house tomorrow?"

And if by dinner time, his chore isn't done, then just don't set him a place at dinner. And quietly but firmly decide not to do anything for him until he does his chores. Occasionally, you might initiate a discussion where you express to him how you *feel* about his nonparticipation.

"I really am upset about your not doing your chores. I feel resentful about having someone here just freeloading. And I'm worried too; I don't understand why you are doing this. Is there something that's upsetting you that you'd like to talk about?"

This is deciding what *you* will do.

Exercise Forty Nine

HAVE PATIENCE DURING THE TRANSITION POWER STRUGGLES

If you have a respectful relationship with your teen and you allow him to truly make his own decisions, then during those rare occasions when you feel that he is making a dangerous decision, you will be able to explain your fear and your insistence that he follow your decision. And he will be fine about going along with it, because he truly knows that you are wiser about the world and have his interests at heart. He will know that this isn't about a power struggle because your relationship isn't about power struggles.

But if you don't allow your teen to make his own life decisions when he would be perfectly capable of doing so, and your relationship is an adversarial one, then during those rare occasions where you feel he is in danger, he won't be able to hear you. He will only hear what he hears every day – you trying to control him.

TWO WEEKS FROM HELL

State changes take time. Parents with fit throwing, out of control toddlers, who decide to take my advice, and take the reins of their 3 year old's life back into their own hands, providing their toddler with boundaries, structure and rhythm, often necessitating that they say "No" to their child, report that there is a transition period where the child rebels with all her might. It is exceedingly difficult for the parent to maintain his strength and authority over the child during these extreme emotional outbursts. The temptation to give in to the old ways, where the child ran the household, is strong. But if the parents stay strong in their stance, the child gets used to it. And they report that their relationship with the child becomes incredibly peaceful, the child is calm, secure and happy for the first time, and the fit throwing becomes a thing of the past.

Now you are making another state change. But this time you

are giving the reins back again. Nevertheless, it will take some time to go through the transition. The temptation to grab those reins and commence your usual parental tirade will be strong. Expect it. Even though your child is old enough now to speak to her consciously about this change, she will be used to a certain way of relating with you. She will be used to doing whatever she feels like until you make her do otherwise. She might expect you to punish her, to be against her, to see her as a child. And it is you, not her, who must be strong and firmly stay in the new relationship structure.

"What are you going to do about it, huh, mom? Punish me?"

"No, I'm not. If you choose to make that choice, then you will have to suffer whatever natural consequences proceed from it. You are old enough now to make your own decisions."

INNER VS. OUTER MOTIVATION

When you cease and desist from ordering your teen around, she will begin to move from outer motivation to inner motivation. Outer motivation means that she is doing her actions because she is forced to by someone else. Inner motivation is where *she decides* to do something. When she is faced with a difficult situation, and she, herself, (even if you are guiding her) goes through the process of considering the pros and cons of each option, and then she chooses one of the options – this is very different from *you* deciding what the best option is and telling her what she must do. In the first scenario, she will be doing it because of her understanding that it is the best choice, despite any attendant discomforts from the choice. In the second scenario, she will be doing it because you made her, and she will blame the discomforts on you, because she never accepted them. She will identify only with the part of her that doesn't want to do it, when actually there is a part of her that does want to do it. If you had let her make the decision herself, she would have also identified with that part of her that does want to do it (because of the fact that it is the best choice).

If that last paragraph gave you a headache, let me say it a different way in terms of Inner Freedom. If you take up the part of the Inner Parent, then she will take up the part of the Inner Child. She won't identify, or become aware of, the Inner Parent that is inside of her. Her Inner Parent won't need to be activated, because you are already doing that job. So she will remain identified with her Inner Child "But I don't feel like doing this." This is called immaturity.

If, instead, you guide her in the process of making the decision, you will help her to first identify with her Inner Child, "So a con of this option is that you don't feel like doing it. Yes, I see that. And what might be a pro?" And now, she can identify with her Inner Parent, "Well, it would be better for me in the long run." Now her Inner Adult (her ego) can make the decision, having taken into account the voices of both the Inner Parent and Child. This is a free decision.

Please note. When the motivation to action is coming from within your teen, the once overwhelming problem of enforcement becomes moot.

FROM ENFORCEMENT TO SUPPORT

Often parents will succeed in allowing their teen to make his own decision, and they might even agree with the decision. But then the teen will lack the life skills to follow through with his intention. When the one year old is learning to walk, we don't just give up on him if he falls again and again. We realize that it takes time to learn new skills. And in the same way, we need to support our older children in learning life skills.

Carol and her parents discussed the problem of her having fallen asleep at school, and rather than punish her, they allowed her to come up with a solution to the problem. She decided to go to bed by 10:30. At 10:30 that night, her dad walks by her room and sees her texting her friends.

Rather than:

"OK young lady, that's it. We tried to deal with you in this new way, but you have totally blown it. I see that we can't trust you. You are grounded."

Try:

"Uh, Carol. I thought you decided to go to bed earlier, but it's 10:30 and I see you are still texting your friends."

"Oh God, Dad, I forgot!"

"Yes, I know it can be hard to remember to implement new intentions. What can you do to prevent this from happening again?"

"Well, let me think about it......hey, my phone has an alarm in it. I can set the alarm to go off at 9:30 every night, and that will remind me to say goodbye to my friends in time to get ready for bed."

"Wow! Great idea! Excellent creative thinking!"

Exercise Fifty

QUOTATION CONTEMPLATION

"The day the child realizes that all adults are imperfect he becomes an adolescent; the day he forgives them, he becomes an adult; the day he forgives himself, he becomes wise."
—Aiden Nowlan

Exercise Fifty One

EXAMINING YOUR TEEN PARENTING SKILLS

If you are parenting a teen, I would suggest the following End of Day Review Exercise for the next two weeks:

Think through your day, remembering your interactions with your teen. For each interaction, consider the following points which were articulated in this exercise. For each time you spoke to your teen in a way you'd like to change, imagine what you wish you had said. You will be practicing a new way of relating imaginally, which will soon begin to manifest in real life.

1. Was the interaction parent to child, or adult to adult? (note – nurturing your teen when he gets into the little child mode is fine…it's wonderful actually). If it was parent to child, how could you have framed it adult to adult?

_____

_____

_____

_____

_____

2. Did you use words like 'allow,' 'should,' or 'must'? How might you have reframed this?

_____

_____

_____

_____

_____

3. Were there decisions you made for him that he'd be safe (i.e. not causing irreparable harm) making himself?

_____

_____

_____

_____

_____

4. Did you put in your opinion, as your opinion, rather than as the 'truth,' or rather than not speaking up? What could you have said?

_____

_____

_____

_____

_____

_____

5. If she made a 'mistake ,' how could you have responded by pointing out natural law, another person's feelings, or your own feelings?

_____

_____

_____

_____

_____

6. If she was violating you, did you act like a doormat, act in a parental critical way? How could you have responded respectfully, to protect your boundaries, as you would to any other adult?

End Of The List

STAGE 3 - brainstorming doable actions

STAGE 4 - putting your actions into your

time system

STAGE 5 - End of Day Review

Exercise Fifty Two

KIDS STAGE 3

Now, using the list you made for each child during Stage 1, for each item, brainstorm some actions you can take to make the changes you desire to manifest.

In Stage 3 you will end up with a list of doable actions, one for each child.

_____

_____

_____

_____

_____

_____

_____

_____

_____

_____

_____

_____

_____

KIDS

STAGE THREE

_____

_____

_____

_____

_____

_____

_____

_____

_____

_____

_____

Exercise Fifty Three

KIDS STAGE 4

Using the list you made in Stage 3, take each doable action and put it on your calendar, schedule, MAL, or To Do List.

See Appendix F.

Exercise Fifty Four

KIDS STAGE 5

In Stage 5 of the End of the List Workshop, you look back over your day and consider whether the action steps you have brainstormed in Stage 3 and are doing in Stage 4 are working for you. If need be, you can brainstorm some new action steps. Or you can contemplate what is keeping you from enacting the action steps. Or you can contemplate what is working well for you and you might want to do more.

This contemplation process is called End of Day Review in EOL, and is facilitated by a 'cheat sheet.' The cheat sheet is updated after every area of EOL (body, house, work, etc) and is comprehensive. If you haven't been doing EOL all the way through, you can consult previous books of EOL, or skip the parts of the End of Day Review cheat sheet that don't pertain to you. The cheat sheet is found in Appendix G.

Exercise Fifty Five

BUT ISN'T THE EGO THE BAD GUY?

In this book I have advocated that parents support the growth of a healthy ego, a healthy Inner Adult, in their children. At this point I feel I need to address the subject of ego, because there seems to be quite a bit of confusion about what the word ego means.

Often the word ego is used to mean egotistical, which isn't exactly what I am referring to when I use the word ego, but I'd like to take the opportunity to address this issue. Egotistical means to have an excessive focus on the individual self, believing that, or attempting to believe that, one's self is superior to other people. "You think you are so great!" Of course, this situation can go to the other extreme too and be just as unhealthy. A person can lack self esteem. The word "pride" is used as a positive attribute, until it becomes excessive. The beliefs that you are better or you are worse than other people are both just a form of separation, of judgment.

We don't want our child to become egotistical, but if looked at on a continuum, with lack of self esteem on the other end, we are aiming for a balance. So be careful of condemning your child for trying to feed his self esteem (as religious/spirituality might suggest) and be careful of following too thoroughly the advice of psychologists who advocate constantly praising your child to "develop self esteem." Gandhi defined humility as being "a whole person, but just one person."

Now I will move on to discussing the word ego in the sense I've used it in this book. I am using it to mean the sense a person acquires, of being a separate self; a separate entity from the rest of the world.

I am going to attempt to describe, as simply as possible, what might be called a psycho-spiritual path of development. And I will try to clear up the confusion about the ego as best I can.

Refer to the Coming Home Path diagram on page 214. This path can be said to have stages of development as follows:

Stage 1 - Ego Formation. A child is born not knowing what is him and what is not him. He is said to be "undifferentiated," or to be identified with everything. To him, he *is* everything. As he grows he begins to make distinctions; this is my body, this is not my body; this is my feeling and that person might not be feeling it; this thought is in my head and a different thought might be in her head, etc. Until the point where he has some identity. He identifies with his body, with his feelings and with his thoughts. In short, his personality. This sense of being somebody separate from his world, is his developed ego.

In this state his thinking is discursive, meaning that wherever his thoughts go, he is dragged behind them, off to Timbuktu and back. And he experiences himself to be victim to his feelings. They just happen to him and there's nothing he can do about it. When his emotions overtake him, his actions can even seem beyond his control. On the Coming Home Path diagram this stage would be depicted as moving up the left side until you reach the Room of the Turn.

Stage 2 - The Split of the Personality. Probably the majority of people never leave stage 1. In stage 2, it occurs to the person that he lives in his body, but he is not his body; he experiences his feelings but he is not his feelings; and he hears the English words of his thoughts floating through his head, but he is not those thoughts. He sees that he is something beyond these things. He is something more timeless. He is the experiencer of these things. The watcher. The witness.

This is beautifully pictorialized in the Wizard of Oz, when, on her path, Dorothy meets her thinking (scarecrow), feeling (tin man), and body (lion). And then she begins to work together with them.

On the The Coming Home Path diagram, this is the Room of the Turn.

At this point the nomenclature changes. We have left the realm of psychology and entered the realm of spirituality/religion. That which we were calling ego, we now call the "Witness," "Pure consciousness," or the "Self" with a capital S. All of a sudden, when we say ego, we aren't referring to the witness anymore, but are referring to our discursive thinking and our out of control feelings which possess us.

See the confusion? Now ego is the bad guy! Now the advice we hear is to annihilate the ego. We are told that it is the ego which keeps us from the spiritual experience we seek.

Well, it gets even more complicated....

Stage 3 - Inner Work. Here, the person begins to do his spiritual work. He learns to focus his mind and to hear his feelings without being slave to them. After years of meditation he succeeds in slowing the mind to the point where it is still. Sometimes people experience this state out of the blue, in what is called a "peak experience," without making any effort, but it is a rare occurrence that this state stays with the person.

This work is done in the Room of Inner Effort on The Coming Home Path.

Stage 4 - Witness. Once the mind can be still, a person can experience his witness, his pure consciousness directly. (I don't think Descartes achieved this stage.) This is often mistaken for being an enlightenment experience. But it is still an experience in duality. There is still the sense of two things being there. There is the witness which is focusing on something else. There is "me" experiencing "that". "I" am seeing inner light. Two things. At some point, it occurs to the person, to become more curious about the witness itself, than about the object of focus. The attention shifts back onto his own consciousness. He tries to be conscious of his own consciousness. An eyeball seeing itself!

If our children don't develop a balanced psyche with a healthy ego, they won't have enough strength in their witness to come to this process. The witness just won't be "there" enough. This witness is none other than that very ego that we developed in the beginning of our life.

A person who can still her mind is most definitely in the Room of Channeling on The Coming Home Path diagram.

So why, then, do the spiritual traditions talk about ego death, going beyond the ego to experience what is truth? The answer to this question lies in Stage 5.

Stage 5 - Enlightenment. When the witness/ego tries to see its own self, it finds that there is nothing there. There is just experience. Not me experiencing that (duality), but just experience only (unity). The sense of separate self vanishes. This is an enlightenment experience.

So when spiritual traditions say that you must go beyond the ego, this is what they mean. It isn't a matter of killing the ego; it is a matter of realizing that the ego isn't really there. On this non-material level of reality, the ego is just a mirage. All that fuss and bother, all that beating your head against the wall, trying to fight against the ego, was just silly.

You can sense the importance of ego in another way. Think back to stage 1. A person starts off in the world identified with every-thing. In a sense, he is one with everything. And in enlighten-ment experience you become one with everything too. But these two experiences are not the same thing. What is different is that in enlightenment experience, you know that you are there, (or at least after it ends you do). The difference between the infant and the enlightened person is the ego.

(Did you hear the one about the Buddhist who went to the hot dog vendor and said "Make me one with everything"?)

After this point, I can't speak from experience. Possibly people can stay in the unity state and walk around on the earth all day. If so, please pardon my ignorance, but it is my experience that it is in coming out of the unity state and regaining my sense of "Jane", that the whole meaning lies. It seems to me that the illusion of "Jane" is what it is all about. Yes, having the unity experience, it becomes obvious that "Jane," my ego, is an illusion. But what a beautiful illusion! How clever! Because what seems to me to be even more beautiful than the unity experience itself, is the appreciation that only an ego can have. It's as if God created the illusion of little separate selves so that there could be appreciation of God.

You must know the feeling I'm speaking of - in those still quiet moments in the night, when you are kissing your child softly, and smelling her, and feeling such a deep love emanating from you to her, and knowing that there is nothing in the world you wouldn't do for her. Isn't there for you, a sense that this moment, this feeling, could not be surpassed in all the world, in all of time? That this is the pinnacle of creation itself? Just this simple and pure and total love from one separate self to another?

So, yes, in the end, for enlightenment experience, we must transcend our egos. But it is a misunderstanding, I believe, to talk about getting rid of the ego. Rather, I prefer to think of the ego as a table. To reach enlightenment we need to stand on this table. From this perspective we can give the ego a bit more due respect, and not fear to support our children in developing a nice strong one.

Exercise Fifty Six

TODAY'S EXERCISE

Close your eyes and visualize your child. Feel your love flowing from your chest, like a beam of gentle light, surrounding the child in a warm glow. You can offer the following prayer to your child:

I am here for you.

My hands are under you to support you.

My hands are on either side of you, encircling you,
to discipline you, to keep you from straying off the path.

My hands caress you, letting you bask in the massage of unconditional love.

My hands are pushing you, teaching you to be independent, and to do your very best.

And when you are ready to walk ahead of me on your own,
I will lower my hands.

But I will always be behind you in case you falter.

I will always love you.

Jane Martin

EOL

STAGE 2 ENCORE

15 PARENTING TECHNIQUES

TO SUPPORT THE HEALTHY DEVELOPMENT OF

THE PREFRONTAL CORTEX

Exercise Fifty Seven

PARENTING FOR A HEALTHY PREFRONTAL CORTEX

As I alluded to earlier, disciplining your child properly is essential to the healthy development of your child's prefrontal cortex (PFC), the most highly evolved part of the brain, the dysfunction of which is associated with most mental health disorders.

Towards a Healthy Prefrontal Cortex

	Function	Mental Health Disorder	15 Ways to Reclaim Health
Relationship with Others	Attunement Empathy Attachment	Attachment Disorder Antisocial P.D. Narcissistic P.D.	End of Day Review
Relationship with the World	Focus Will Planning Problem Solving Decision making Meaning making	Learning problems ADD/ADHD Dependent Personality	Unstructured play Order Discipline Nutrition Touch Birth Screen exposure
Relationship with Self	Emotional regulation	Bipolar Disorder, Anxiety and phobia disorders, ODD/conduct disorder, Depression,	Rhythm . Emotional Intelligence and healing
	Impulse control	OCD, impulse control disorder, addictions	Stress bust-redefine success - simplify
	Ego	DID, BPD, autism, psychotic disorders	Sensory integration Touch Movement
Relationship with Transcendent	Morality Intuition Transcendence	Still not enlightened!	Awe and reverence

You now have a clear idea of how to discipline your child. But before you consider discipline, an issue that arises only when a child exhibits some undesirable behavior, it seems fair to first consider the cause of the undesirable behavior.

For example, Sam, a four-year-old boy, is hopping out of his seat, moving and making noise during a theater production. His mother becomes annoyed at him and speaks harshly. Sam gets the message that he is "bad," yet he can't make his own body stay still. I sit one row behind him and can't help but smell the strong perfumes from the fabric softener his mother uses on his laundry. It occurs to me that possibly poor Sam actually can't sit still. Possibly the dpha-terpineol or the camphor or some other toxic chemical used in the fabric softener is irritating his central nervous system. If I were breathing those toxic chemicals all day, I'd be hopping out of my seat too! Dealing with Sam's behavior as a discipline problem would be unfair and unproductive. If a child doesn't feel well, he won't behave well.

I recently gave a workshop with Dr Ginsburg, the medical doctor at Volition Wellness Center where I work, entitled "Raising a Healthy Child." Together we were looking at the exponential rise in the rates of physical and mental health disorders in the last 50 years. The list was long – cancer, autism, autoimmune disease, diabetes, obesity, and the situation is similar with mental health disorders. It is estimated that by the time today's children reach18yrs, 40% of them will be diagnosed with a mental health disorder. This is almost double the rate of our generation.

Working together with Dr Ginsberg, combining the lens of psychology and medicine, we began to take a broader view of 'what is going on!!??' Then we began to list some changes in the way people have been parenting, and the changes in the environment that children are exposed to over the last 50 years. Of course this list is very long too, and I will be noting some of it below.

In looking at the mental health disorders, I began to notice that most of them were associated with problems in the function of just one part of the brain called the prefrontal cortex (PFC). The PFC sits right behind the forehead. It is the most highly evolved part of the brain, and is responsible for the most uniquely human qualities, such as our sense of self, will, attention, empathy, planning, decision making, impulse control, emotional regulation, etc. I began to research this and found that, in fact, most of the disorders listed in the DSM-IV, the manual that categorizes mental disorders, were connected to some dysfunction in the PFC when measured by fMRI or other brain scanning techniques.

Once I noticed this, I began to look at the prescriptions for mental health and healing that I have been suggesting to my child patients' parents for many years, and I realized that they all were exercising the PFC functions in some way.

It appears that the cultural changes in parenting that have occurred over the last 50 years in our society, have inadvertently removed the support that our children's prefrontal cortices need for healthy development. This section of this book is to give you a list of ways you can bring these important supports back into your child's life.

Consider each suggestion and whether you might make some changes in your child's life to enable him to feel well so he can behave well. If you find something you'd like to change, put it on your Stage 1 list.

Exercise Fifty Eight

1. END OF DAY REVIEW

One of the most important functions of the PFC is to help a person attune and attach to another person. There is a whole body of psychology called attachment theory. This research has studied the way that babies bond to their caregivers. A healthy attachment is predictive of healthy relationships and psychological health.

How is healthy attachment created? Through spending time paying attention to each other. Through eye contact. Through being aware of what your child is feeling and thinking. This is called attunement. Both attachment and attunement are functions of the PFC.

By setting aside 15 minutes per day to pay attuned attention to your child by doing End of Day Review, you are supporting the healthy development of her PFC. You are filling her need to be seen, to be understood, to be cared about.

Another crucial capacity of the PFC is empathy. During EOD Review, you are demonstrating empathy to your child. This is how he will learn to empathize with others. A 2010 study at the University of Michigan showed a 40% drop after 2000 in the capacity for college freshman to have empathy. The escalating rates of crime, bullying, and oppression worldwide are a testament to this crisis.

Over the past 50 years, parents' and children's schedules have become more and more filled. The time that parents used to spend naturally, in attuned attention with their children has decreased. American parents pay on average 3.5 minutes per day of attuned attention to their children. Contrast this with the average 7 hours that the 8-18 year child spends looking at a screen, TV, computers etc. At this point, it is important that we intentionally put this time back into their schedules. It is crucial.

End of Day Review supports the first group of PFC functions, attachment, attunement, and empathy. See appendix G.

Exercise Fifty Nine

2. UNSTRUCTURED PLAY

Unstructured play is one of those things that has been quietly lost from our children's lives when no one was looking. Back in the day, in the 1960's after school and weekends, kids were told "go out and play." You'd go outside and there'd be a herd of kids to play with. Now I don't see herds. I rarely see kids outside playing at all. Their lives are so busy. They are so scheduled that there is very little time for unstructured play.

Recently I had a therapy session with a teen who was losing her father. He is the only source of warmth in her life. She is overwhelmed emotionally. That day, she had awakened at 6:45 am, gone to school, done a sport, went to tutoring, came to me, and then was going home to 2 hours of homework. Where in her day was time to even process this grief, much less have time for creativity? She was so overloaded, she just put her head on my lap, I turned down the lights, we spoke softly, I rubbed her back, so she could just cry and integrate all of this.

One brain researcher, Douglas Gerwin, Ph.D., contends that unstructured play is a prerequisite to cognitive function, especially executive function. Why? Imagine your child approaching you, saying, "We're bored. There's nothing to do," and you, being wise, and knowing that boredom is the mother ground for creativity, respond, "That's hard. I bet you wish you could think of something so awesome to do!"

Your child then stands there thinking. Creativity. She's intuiting – this is a PFC function. She has created an abstract vision, it's not concrete. In industrialized countries, 65% of adults can't think abstractly. In order to get that vision to manifest, she has to focus on it – another PFC function, make a plan, make decisions, problem solve, and push through with the force of her will , all PFC executive functions. If you think about it, aren't these the functions that are necessary for leadership?

Jane Martin

Prefrontal Cortex Functions

Focus

Attachment

Emotional Regulation

Empathy

Impulse Control

Intuition

Morality

Ego

Transcendence

Decision making

Problem Solving

Planning

Awe and Reverence

Willpower

The best thing to me about unstructured play, is that the children fail. They try to create and they fail. And they fail again. And no parent is there to tell them that this is not ok. They take it in stride. They just naturally pick themselves up and try again. You don't see a one year old learning to walk, and they fall, and then just sit on the ground and say, 'oh forget it, I can't walk.' No! They try again, and they learn that failure is what happens on the way to success. In our society which gives kids a trophy for just showing up, they don't learn to work hard. When I see art projects hanging in the school hallway that took the kids ½ hour to produce, I feel sad. I was grateful that my kids had projects that took them weeks to finish. Knitting, or cross-stitching, or carving.

When my kids were growing up, I had a home business and worked a lot. They had plenty of time for unstructured play. I remember reading an article in Mothering Magazine entitled "Benign Neglect." It made me feel less guilty about ignoring my kids! I remember one day, I looked out the window and saw my kids and the neighbors up on top of the swingset. They had decided to make a way to get from our yard to the neighbors yard without going around on the street. They had a huge plank of wood and were nailing it to the top of the swingset so they could walk across it over the fence into the other yard. The only thing holding up the wood was a few nails. Of course, as soon as they let go of the wood, it sank down. Failure. Then they decided to dig a tunnel under the fence. After a few hours of that futile effort, they decided to cut a path through the woods. They lay slate and planted flowers, and 15 years later, the 'fairy path' still exists. Minus the flowers.

It seems to me that it's this kind of play, that allows for creative visioning, planning, problem solving, and failing, that is the precursor for the successful ventures that my children are engaged in today in their adult lives.

The American Academy of Pediatrics issued a report in 2006 stating that unstructured free play is essential for children's development. This used to be a natural part of life, but now we might have to intentionally provide time for it

Exercise Sixty

3. ORDER

"The basis for inner security and a sense of order, as well as the regular and unquestioning performance of duty, is an orderly environment with a fixed pattern of life. Unconscious imitation of word and deed forms the child's later receptivity for conscious moral teaching."
—Bernard Lievegoed, *Phases of Childhood*

Please note that in anthroposophy, which is Lievegoed's discipline, "duty" and "moral teaching" do not mean duties and morals given by society to someone, but rather to a man's free inner duty and morals, i.e. having the freedom from being compelled either by his own whims or by society's constraints, and being able to live the way he chooses to live. So Lievegoed is saying that it will help our children develop this inner strength, if we provide an orderly environment for them.

Imagine walking into a house that is cluttered and dirty; where many items are in need of repair. Imagine you have lost your keys and are frantically searching through the mess to find them. Feel - in your body. Be with this feeling in your mind and in your body.

Now imagine a clean, quiet home. Where everything is in its place. Where someone has intentionally created beauty. Feel your body now.

Children feel this difference too.

My suggestion is to make one big list of everything that needs to be done to make your home the way you'd like it to be, with every possession having a proper place to "live." Schedule a certain amount of time every week to devote to creating an orderly, beautiful home, and simply go down that list during the scheduled time. Gradually your house will become orderly. What a relief! Even if it takes a few months, you will be so glad you did it. You will, of course, need to include on your schedule the chores necessary to keep it orderly, such as doing the daily tidying, cleaning etc. Book 2 of EOL – Creating a Pleasant Home, guides you through this process.

Our brains are wired to become aroused at novelty. If you think of our ancestors on the savannah, just doing their work - anything that was there in their environment since yesterday was probably safe. But if something new showed up, it could possibly be dangerous. They would become aroused, and their lower brain functions, their reptilian brain, their instincts, would kick in. All their attention would go to making sure that this new thing wasn't going to harm them. If it was dangerous they'd run or they'd fight. Fight or flight.

So novelty wires our brain down, and calm wires our brain up to the higher level of the PFC.

This is very evident in that pregnant mothers whose environments were unsafe tend to have babies whose brains are wired down to the reptilian brain, and mothers whose environments were calm and safe, tend to have babies with larger frontal lobes.

Order and rhythm create calm environments, where children can know what to expect, and relax into that.

Exercise Sixty One

4. RHYTHM

Children, to feel safe and calm, need rhythm. Where order gives all the physical items in your life an intentional place to live in space, rhythm gives all your activities an intentional place to live in time. You can do your children (and yourself) a huge favor by writing out a simple weekly schedule. Follow the step by step procedure in Appendix B, using the grid in Appendix E. It brings a wonderful feeling of security when a child knows he will wake up at the same time each day, eat meals and nap at the same time, and go through a set bedtime ritual the same way each day. Each week can have a rhythm too - Monday is shopping, Tuesday is playdate day, etc. And even the year has its own rhythms, with holidays and seasonal activities. The more these activities can remain regular and traditional for the child, the greater will be his sense of belonging and safety in the world. Rhythm provides a safe base on which a child can feel supported as he reaches out to grow into new life experiences.

As with order, this calm can help the brain wire up to the PFC, rather than down to the reptilian brain because of excessive novelty.

Exercise Sixty Two

5. DISCIPLINE

Discipline gives us the four skills so that we can make free decisions. This is an executive function of the PFC. The bulk of this book is describing the how-to's of discipline.

Exercise Sixty Three

6. NUTRITION

The brain is a physical organ of the body, and so, of course, it will be affected by our physical health.

Try to recall what your child ate over the past few days, or if you can't, then keep track for the next few. Check to be sure she eats at least one fruit per day, something green (green lollipops don't count), and some protein every few hours. It is quite possible for a child who has unlimited access to junk food to be undernourished. I'm not suggesting that you rigidly control everything your child eats - but using the idea of choice within limits, just limit the junk food by not having it around the house. According to a study by Adele Davis, author of Let's Have Healthy Children, given free access to wholesome foods, a child will eat a perfectly well rounded diet on his own. He may eat 7 eggs in one day and 6 apples the next, but over a week it will be well rounded. If you feel your child's diet could be improved, I suggest having as your challenge to slowly move to a more whole foods diet and gradually decrease the amount of empty calories without your child noticing. Make a game of it for yourself. Don't say anything, just do it, and do it gradually. Can you outsmart her? I'm making this a game, but I don't mean to understate the importance of avoiding power struggles about food. Don't fret that you can't control what your child eats elsewhere until you have done what you can do – by offering only healthy food in your home.

Exercise Sixty Four

7. TOXINS

"Around the world, one hundred thousand synthetic chemicals are now on the market. Each year one thousand new substances are introduced, most of them without adequate testing and review....Between 1940 and 1982, production of synthetic materials increased roughly 350 times, and billions of pounds of man-made chemicals poured into the environment, exposing humans, wildlife, and the planetary system to countless compounds never before encountered."
—*Theo Colborn, et al., Our Stolen Future*

"All children today are very much at risk from the chemicalization of our environment. Parents of school-age kids grew up during the post-World-War-II chemical revolution, taking plastics and other synthetic products for granted. Although these kids' grandparents knew a world without TV, detergents, fabric softeners, synthetic fabrics, and petroleum-based pesticides, the parents did not, and tend to use such products as if they had always existed, rarely questioning their safety."
—*Lynn Lawson, Staying Well in a Toxic World*

See Appendix H for a checklist of common toxins in your house and food. Toxins that can't be excreted through the body's detox pathways are stored in the fat cells until such time as the detox pathways become clear. The brain is mostly fat cells.

Many commonly prescribed medications can have significant behavioral side effects. Similarly, certain chronic medical conditions, such as hormonal imbalances or brain dysfunction can prevent children from behaving how you'd like. In fairness to the child, before we judge him as "bad," we must ask "Can he behave?" If you suspect that your child has behavior problems linked to drugs or physical illness, take him to a doctor.

Being that most medical doctors are unaware of these issues, you might seek out a naturopathic, or functional medicine doctor, or other alternative professional.

Exercise Sixty Five

8. BIRTH

If you are pregnant, you might want to research about common obstetrical interventions and their effects on the child. Be sure interventions are done for the good of your child and not for the protection or convenience of a hospital. Skyrocketing rates of unnatural birth interventions such as, ultrasound, amniocentesis, epidurals, use of drugs, pitocin, amniotomy, electronic fetal monitors, eye drops, cesarean sections, circumcisions, vaccinations and more, make many parents wary and want to learn for themselves. A good book to read is <u>Optimal Care in childbirth: The case for a physiologic approach</u>, by Hence Goer and Amy Romano. Or check out <u>A Good Birth, A Safe Birth</u> by Diana Korte.

Exercise Sixty Six

9. SCREEN EXPOSURE

Much information has been recently disseminated about the detrimental effects of screen exposure from TV, video games, computers etc. Besides keeping the child inactive and preventing the usual developmental activities from occurring, exposure to electronic stimuli directly affects the brain. The DSM, which is the manual for mental health disorders, lists Internet Addiction Disorder (IAD) for further study because the phenomenon is too new to include it now, but this listing shows the extent of concern about this emerging problem. Prevalence of IAD in U.S., according to the AMA is approx 12% of video game users. A 2012 study in China showed brain effects in adolescents with IAD similar to alcoholics and drug addicts. A 2002 study in London by Koepp et al., found video game playing doubled the dopamine levels in the brain, which could be an explanation for gaming's addictive nature.

Given this information it may be wise for parents to monitor and limit their children's computer use. The AMA recommends no more than one to two hours per day.

For more information read The Children of Cyclops: The Influence of Television Viewing on the Developing Human Brain, by Keith Buzzell. Or Four Arguments for the Elimination of Television, by Jerry Mander.

Exercise Sixty Seven

10. EMOTIONAL ENVIRONMENT

Children take in emotions directly, undigested. It doesn't matter if they know or understand what is going on, they feel what you feel.

My suggestion is to feel into what your emotional environment is like. Are emotions repressed on one hand, or expressed out of control on the other?

How about the marital relationship?

How are conflicts resolved?

If the way emotions are handled in your family doesn't feel healthy to you, there are many tools available. Look online to learn about Nonviolent Communication, or Imago Couples Counseling. You can work on your relationship skills yourself, or see a therapist for support. Don't be shy. There's no shame in this. Most couples have these problems. There is movement in this country to bring Social Emotional Learning into the school systems. It's kind of curious when you consider that we learn calculus in school, which we use, umm, never. But we don't learn things like, how to deal with our emotions, or resolve conflict, or make decisions, which we need to do every day! The EOL book "Emotions – An Owners Manual" teaches clear approaches to hearing and using our emotions.

In the discussion of discipline, I discussed how to handle emotional outbursts. Here I want to briefly discuss something else that can adversely affect your child's ongoing behavior- a suppressive emotional environment. I work with Breath Therapy clients who, as children, were shamed or forbidden to cry or to express anger or fear. When emotions can't be expressed, the person must tense against the expression, causing chronic muscular tension known in bodypsychotherapy as "armor." This tension follows them through life, limiting their potential to experience life fully. There is a vast difference between teaching a child to express emotion in a constructive socially acceptable way, and forcing him to "behave" by suppressing his emotions. You may want to speak with your spouse about supporting each other in a new way of handling your child's emotions.

Another inquiry is to consider if your family holds unresolved conflict. None of us is perfect. No marriage is without conflict. Your child will encounter conflict in her life. Conflict isn't a problem for children. The question is: what do you want her to learn about how to best deal with conflict? When a child sees you and your spouse constructively and respectfully resolving your differences, she learns a valuable skill. On the other hand, if conflict goes unresolved, the child will walk around feeling tense and uncomfortable. The conflict resolution model of HowtoFeel-NiceWithAllFolks works just as well with spouses!

And lastly, consider, or better yet, ask friends, about the level of anxiety in the family. When parents are experiencing anxiety, and are overly cautious about a child, the child often picks up this nervous feeling and makes it her own. While we want to be safe, there is also a downside to being overprotective. It's hard sometimes to see this for ourselves, so asking a friend for their impression of your family could be helpful.

Exercise Sixty Eight

11. STRESS BUST – REDEFINE SUCCESS – SIMPLIFY

"To allow oneself to be carried away by a multitude of conflicting concerns, to surrender to too many demands, to commit oneself to too many projects - is to succumb to the violence of our times."
—*Thomas Merton*

The film documentary Race to Nowhere, makes clear our society's unconscious acceptance of a standard for children that is not only largely unattainable, but holds the finish line so far out that children feel pressure and stress and often lose their passion in their efforts to reach it. The finish line itself – that ivy league education – upon close examination, may not even be what we are wanting our children to attain, nor what will make them happy. The children's book Hope for the Flowers, by Trina Paulus, depicts a caterpillar who buys in to his society's myth, and tries to reach the top of a caterpillar pillar. Stepping on everyone's heads, always tense in competition, the caterpillar finally reaches the top, to find that there is nothing there but more caterpillars. Seeing a butterfly, well... you can guess the rest.

Take a moment and really consider what you want for your children. What are your values? What are theirs? Are the activities you choose for them in line with these values? Remembering that everything you sign up for, everything you commit to, has a cost – and that cost is the time. Be sure to hold the value of downtime, ease of life, and simplicity in your mind when making these decisions. Even when purchasing items, you are not only giving up money, but the time to deal with them, and the space in your house. Be sure to value that item against the value of simplicity and ease as well.

My husband and I used to own the Natural Baby Catalog which sold wooden, and natural toys. I was asked to write an article for the Amish magazine Plain about toys. I took a poll of some kids asking what their favorite toy was. I started with my older daughter, Julia, who replied "Lily" (my younger daughter). Lily answered "Daddy." This wasn't going well, being that I was a toy merchant. The article pretty much said that toys are really not necessary for kids, but if you were going to buy toys, stick with very simple toys that the child must 'imagine into,' such as blocks, or a basket of colored silk squares, or simple woolen dolls, or a ball. Fancy plastic toys lose their appeal very quickly and end up cluttering up the house. For children's schedules and environments, less can be more!

Exercise Sixty Nine

12. SENSORY OVERLOAD – RECLAIM DARK AND QUIET

In discussing the Raising a Healthy Child workshop, and asking the question about what has changed in children's environments, one of the biggest changes is increase in sensory input. For two million years, between 7:00 and 9:00 at night, it got dark. But in the last couple of generations, this darkness, the quiet rest for our eyes and souls, has been lost. National Geographic's November 2008 magazine hosted an article, Our Vanishing Night. This interruption in earth's natural cycles is affecting many species, including us. We know that children who sleep with a night light, have a higher incidence of needing glasses. We know that light affects our hormones. When it gets dark, our body produces melatonin. That makes us sleepy. It's easier to put the kids to bed! In the morning, the light stimulates the production of serotonin, the happy hormone.

Our eyes weren't designed to look directly at light. They were designed for light that is bouncing off of things. 7 hours / day looking at a screen, which is backlit overstimulating our brain.

We know that when senses are overstimulated, they harden, they become dulled.

I noticed Sesame street has changed. When my son was little, it was slow and quiet. Ernie and Bert. Now they flash neon short clips, with brash sounds. I did a workshop and one participant worked for CTN. I asked her about Sesame Street, and she confirmed that yes, they did a focus group and found that they were no longer able to sustain children's attention, so they changed the format to startle them more. Wiring down.

It's the same deal with sound. When does your child hear silence. They used to hear birds chirping, wind in the trees, crickets, now what do they hear? Traffic, ipods, TV, planes, leaf blowers?

Exercise Seventy

13 and 14. TOUCH AND MOVEMENT

Light touch and comfortable warmth lead to increases in oxytocin and endorphins that enhance social bonds through an association with a feeling of well-being. Touch also leads to mild sedation, decreases in blood pressure, and aids in autonomic regulation and cardiovascular health. (Knox & Uvnas-Moberg, 1998; Weller & Feldman, 2003)

Where sound and light have increased over time, touch and movement have been quietly lost. I believe a major problem in our society is that our culture discourages touch. Babies used to be carried all day on their parents' moving bodies, constantly receiving tactile and olfactory stimulation. Now we place them in plastic carriers away from our bodies. They used to sleep in the same beds as their parents so they were touched all night long. Now we isolate them from us in their own room in their own bed. The crib is a very new experiment evolutionarily speaking.

And nursing, which provides beautiful touch, is now only experienced by half of the American babies. Indeed, society is becoming increasingly afraid of touch; teachers, therapists, and other caregivers are warned against touching children for fear of lawsuits.

With this in mind, just reverse the trend. Pick up your child, invite him onto your lap. (My son is 21 and he still fits - he just leans back against me while he watches TV. Aaaah.) During bedtime offer a back rub. If you are sitting on the rocking chair, child in lap, and your thoughts are telling you that you are "wasting time," just know that there is nothing in the universe that could be more productive or more full of beauty and love! Know that this sense of being cared for will live inside your child for his whole life.

Touch may be the primary building block of consciousness. One of the important functions of the PFC is to house, to a great degree, our ego. Ego means sense of self. 'I am here.' 'I am a separate identity from everything else in the world.' That's why I have touch listed on the above PFC chart next to the function of 'ego.'

Touch may be integral to the development of ego as it is the first building block. The baby's sense of touch streams into the brain and he develops what neuroscientist, Antonio Damasio, calls a 'felt body sense.' 'Here is me, and here is not me. I'm not all this other stuff, I am this body.' Without this basic building block fully formed, our children may be building their egos on a faulty foundation. If the foundation block is off, it affects all the blocks on top of it. Many teachers report an increase in children needing body contact. Boys are crashing more and more into each other and into things in order to feel their bodies. Some teachers are making large dolls filled with sand to let the children lie under, so they can feel their own bodies and calm down.

The research is there but most therapists don't learn about bodypsychotherapy. But this is vitally important.

And movement is lost too. Children used to run around all day. It is very recent in history that they began to go to school and sit in a desk all day. At least they used to have recess but even that is getting cut by many schools. This isn't natural for them.

Exercise Seventy One

15. AWE AND REVERENCE

And my last suggestion is to create a small space for reverence.

33% of American's identify as spiritual but not religious according to a Gallup poll. I'm not saying to go to church, but don't throw the baby out with the bathwater. My suggestion is to take a few minutes each day – a grace before meals, lighting a candle before bed and singing a song, or saying a prayer or poem. You don't have to do anything to create awe in a child. It is there naturally. Just make a space for it to come out.

And I want to give a shout out to parents who create lovely holiday traditions. It doesn't matter what the tradition is. It's just so nice for the child when the family is together, and there is some attention given to something divine, or nature, or just something larger than our lives. This is also a PFC function, and I believe it is a precursor to transcendence when they are older.

So, these are some ways of parenting to consider which can strongly support your child's wellbeing. If your child feels well, he can behave well.

Don't worry if you've been parenting in a way that's different than I suggest here. No parent is perfect, and no child needs a perfect parent. In fact, our brains are malleable for our whole lives. Scientists used to think that our brains, and our personalities were formed and unchangeable once we exited childhood, but new brain studies show neuroplasticity throughout the lifespan. You can always improve starting from right now.

Exercise Seventy Two

CONSIDERING THE 15 PARENTING METHODS FOR YOUR CHILD

For today's exercise, consider each of the 15 suggested parenting methods, and add anything pertinent to your Stage 3 list of action steps. Then add the actions to your time system.

Jane Martin

APPENDICES

Appendix A

PLAYING CATCHUP WITH EOL

This book is the 4th in of a series of 9 books, each concentrating on one of the key aspects of your life, which together describe and explain "The End of the List Workshop" (EOL), a series of daily 10 minute psychospiritual exercises designed to help you elevate your life. If you have read the previous books, you can certainly skip this appendix, which is designed to give newcomers the basic ideas of EOL.

The overall goal of EOL is to help you move around "The Coming Home Path," (see diagram below) a developmental continuum that is the theoretical basis of my work.

Moving around The Coming Home Path is a 5 stage process.

Stage 1. Creating a clear vision of how you'd like this area of your life to be.

Stage 2. Learning relevant principles that relate to the area you'd like to elevate.

Stage 3. Brainstorming actions you can take to manifest your vision and make it a reality.

Stage 4. Putting each of those actions into practice, using a time system consisting of a schedule, a to do list, a calendar, and a Morning Affirmation List.

Stage 5. Using contemplative review to examine whether your brain stormed ideas are working or need revision.

These 5 Stages are applied sequentially to each of the 9 areas of your life. Each of the 9 books of EOL helps you apply these 5 stages to one of the 9 areas of life. The books are:

BODY – Time and Body
HOUSE – Creating a Pleasant Home
LIFE'S WORK – Finding Your Passion and Manifesting It
KIDS – An Owner's Manual
LIFE PARTNER – Relationships with Intention
COMMUNITY – Holding Hands
EMOTIONS –An Owner's Manual
INTELLECT – A Brain Owner's Manual
SPIRITUALITY – Keep Your Ego

This 4th book will provide relevant principles about raising children, and will give you exercises to help you through each of the 5 stages. In Stage 1 you will vision what you'd like to create with respect to your children, and create some goals. In Stage 2 you will learn some theory. In Stage 3 you will brainstorm actions you might take to help your vision to manifest. Stage 4 requires the use of a time system onto which you will write your intentions, so that you can remember to consistently enact them at the appropriate time.

In this book I provide a basic skeleton of the time system used in EOL; if you need further help you can refer to the first EOL book entitled Time and Body. Appendix B gives you instructions to develop a weekly schedule, and Appendix F gives you instructions to use the rest of the time system. And Stage 5, a contemplative review, is done using an exercise called End of Day Review. A basic outline for this process is in Appendix G. For a more thorough explanation, see the Time and Body book.

The Coming Home Path Diagram on page 214 illustrates a sequence of energy states – ways to live and feel inside yourself, and ways to view and interpret the world. The goal of EOL is to help you move through these energy states, or Rooms.

I am assuming that to some degree you are beginning in the first Room of Hell, and are experiencing some chaos, suffering or lack of power. Maybe your child is depressed and you don't know what to do, or maybe she is out of control.

The exercises in this book will help you to move into the Room of Outer Effort and start to take control of the situation. You will first gain understanding of the psychological workings of your child, and then begin to formulate intentions on how to change. Maybe you will decide to say no when your daughter wants to stay up late. On the other hand, maybe you will decide to consider your son's desires more when making decisions about his life.

As you carry out your intentions, your child, and your relationship with her will change. You will be able to move through the Room of the Turn and feel a sense of Ok'ness, of Free Will.

Then, once the situation is under control, you can move into the Room of Inner Effort and begin to relax, to let go of the tight control and go with the flow a bit more. Your daughter won't be fighting you about going to bed because it will become routine. Your efforts to consider your son's wishes will become a matter of habit and no longer require effort from you. Your daughter will be better behaved because she'll get enough sleep. Your son will come out of his depression. As happens in the Room of Inner Effort, you'll be able to accept the natural imperfections of life and of your child and still feel ok inside.

And finally, as you move into the Room of Channeling, you will just experience the divine joy of loving your gorgeous child; the wonderful enjoyment of serving him, and feel gratitude for the opportunity to experience one of life's most fulfilling gifts – being a parent.

For a more thorough explanation of the Coming Home Path, see the first book Time and Body, and its applications in all 9 EOL books.

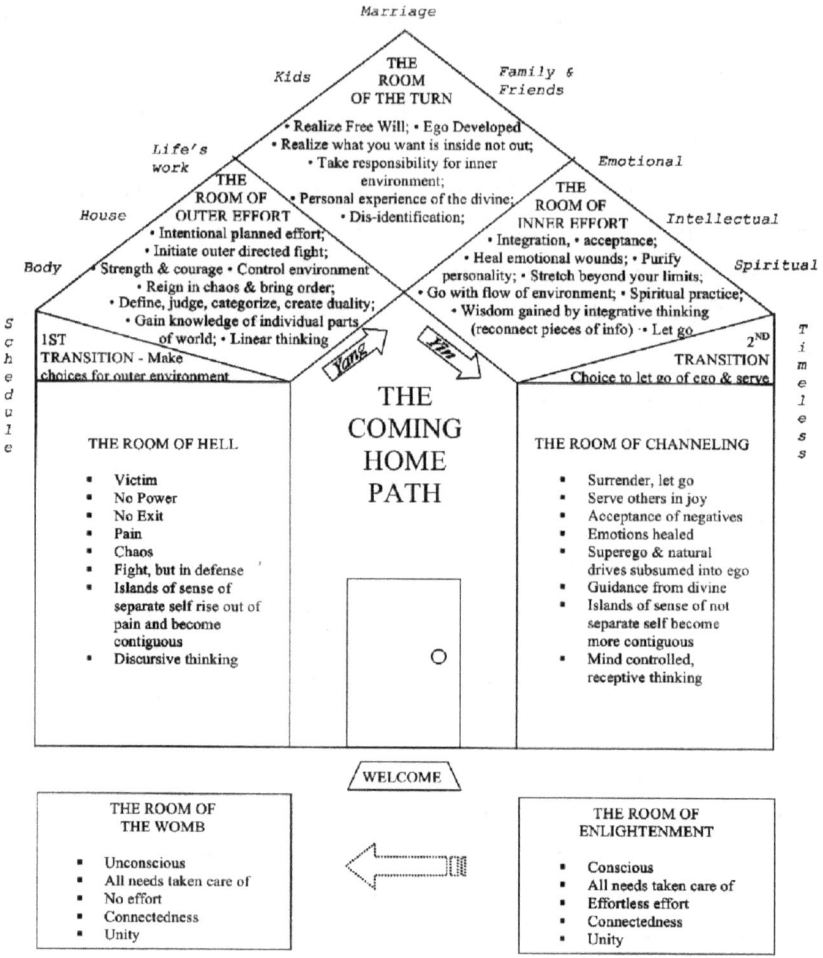

Appendix B

MAKING A LIFE SCHEDULE

WARNING. USE PENCIL!

The first step in developing your time system is to make a weekly schedule. Here are step-by-step instructions to help you make it. Use the grid at the end of this exercise. Fill in your intentions for what you choose to do with the 168 hours per week that you are allotted by the Universe. It is true that this is all you get. You can pretend there are more, that time is unlimited, but, in fact, there are only 168 hours. You may as well live them as you *choose* to live them, rather than letting fate and happenstance choose for you. Most of us find that when we let happenstances choose for us, that we end up dissatisfied with our lives.

1. NON-NEGOTIABLES First you put into your weekly schedule the non-negotiable stuff, like going to work, driving kids, and classes.

Here's how to put on your job, if you leave the house at 8:30 and return at 12:30 (i.e. don't forget to include drive time.) Be sure to clearly delineate beginning and ending times with a line.

	Monday	Tuesday	Wed
6:00			
7:00			
8:00	WORK	WORK	
9:00			
10:00			

2. MORNING AFFIRMATION LIST (MAL), Next put on a time (2 minutes tops) to read your MAL. This is simply a list of reminders of your intentions. They are the kinds of intentions which you don't know exactly when you will do them - i.e. they can't go on your calendar, or To Do List, or schedule. They are things like - improve posture, speak with kindness, every time little Johnny has a fit do such and such. When you get to the "Read MAL" part of your schedule, just read through the list. If you do it every day, the intentions will stay with you. Right now you might have nothing on the list, but you will soon.

3. CALENDAR and IN BOX, Next, put on 5 -10 minutes per day to check your calendar and do your in box. A good time to do this is every morning or every evening. You are basically getting a picture

of your day, you can resolve any time conflicts, make choices, and/ or prioritize what you want to do that day. If you don't have a time on your schedule to look at your calendar, then the system won't work. You'll put a reminder on your calendar, but forget to see it. In the EOL book Creating a Pleasant Home there is a system to do your inbox, entitled "How to do Your Desk." For now, once your inbox papers are processed, take your To Do List and prioritize it.

4. END OF DAY REVIEW, Put on 30 minutes to do End of Day Review. Find a quiet time; you need to be able to go inside undistracted. Appendix G will explain how to do it. This is also the time you will do the daily EOL Exercises.

5. TO DO LIST, Assign time to do your to do list. You'll need a good hunk of time 2-4 hours once per week, plus an hour every day is a good starting point. Increase or decrease as the length of your To Do List dictates. You'll do the To Do List in a prioritized way, starting from the 1's and proceeding down in descending order of importance.

6. TIDY, Schedule 10-15 minutes per day to tidy your house. If you want to make an investment to decrease this amount of time in the long run, try making a note to your family members on what you find, i.e. "Tom's dirty socks found on kitchen table." "Suzie's bathroom light left on."

7. BUFFER, If stress reduction is important to you, you might schedule in a buffer of half hour to hour per day to account for unexpected things, incoming calls, slowness, etc. Some people may need this time to just lie down.

8. MEDITATION, If you are at a point in your life where having a direct experience of transcendence is important to you, I suggest

scheduling in 20 - 60 minutes for doing meditation. By meditation I don't mean contemplation, or any exercise where thinking is going on. You may want to schedule a time for CONTEMPLATION as well. End of Day Review is a time of contemplation in itself.

9. REALITY, Schedule in the daily stuff like:

MEALS
CLEANING
EXERCISE
PAY BILLS
SHOWER
WATER PLANTS
COOK
LAUNDRY
MAKE BEDS
HELP/HUG KIDS
SHOPPING
TAKE PILLS/MEDS
GO ON DATES
RUN/EMPTY DISHWASHER
GET PHONE MESSAGES

10. INNER CHILD FOOD, Is there enough pleasure on your schedule to keep your Inner Child happy? You need pleasure. It's as important to care for yourself as it is to care for anyone else. How about a monthly massage? A bath? Time on the hammock. Time to read useless novels? A time to eat your favorite food, or visit a coffeehouse with a friend, or play Frisbee, or.........

11. CONCENTRATED TIME with SPOUSE and EACH CHILD 1/2 hour/day at bedtime for each kid is nice. Or for teens, time after school to do homework or talk.

Note: If a day is sometimes spent one way and sometimes spent another, for example a class every other week, you can draw a vertical line down the day and create two different schedules for that day.

TOMORROW, GIVE YOUR SCHEDULE A TRY. FOLLOW ALONG WITH YOUR SCHEDULE THROUGHOUT THE DAY.

IF LIFE DOESN'T HAPPEN THE WAY YOU PLANNED IT, THAT'S OK! PLEASE DON'T EXPECT IT TO.

PAY ATTENTION TO WHAT REALLY HAPPENS SO YOU CAN TWEAK YOUR SCHEDULE.

REMEMBER, YOU USED PENCIL. AT END OF DAY REVIEW TIME TOMORROW NIGHT, MAKE ANY CHANGES YOU LIKE TO YOUR SCHEDULE.

Appendix C

MORNING AFFIRMATION LIST

Appendix D

TO DO LIST

_____

_____

_____

_____

_____

_____

_____

_____

_____

_____

_____

_____

_____

_____

_____

_____

_____

Appendix E

SCHEDULE

	Monday	Tuesday	Wednesday	Thursday	Friday	Saturday
6:00						
7:00						
8:00						
9:00						
10:00						
11:00						
12:00						
1:00						
2:00						
3:00						
4:00						
5:00						
6:00						
7:00						
8:00						
9:00						
10:00						

Appendix F

USING THE TIME SYSTEM

In Stage 3 you've made a list of actions that you would like to do in order to elevate your life. Each of these intentions can be written on one of four places – your schedule, your to do list, your calendar, or your Morning Affirmation List. Then you will remember to do them at the time you intend to do them.

If the action is to be done 'every,' as in every Tuesday, or every day, write it on your schedule.

If the action is to be done on a specified date, write it on your calendar.

If the action is to be done one time and then it's finished, and you just want to do it the next time you get a chance, write it on your to do list.

If the action can't be tied to a time, in other words, you want to do it all the time, such as 'sit up straighter,' or do it when cued by something else, such as 'whenever Tommy sneezes,' so that it must be something that you keep in your memory, write it on your Morning Affirmation List.

Since you have written on your schedule to read your Morning Affirmation List, you will take a few seconds every day to read it and remind yourself of these intentions. Since you've allotted time in your schedule to do your to do list, the actions on this list will manifest (I strongly suggest prioritizing this list), and since you wrote it on your schedule to check your calendar, these action items will happen as well. All that remains is for you to wake up and begin living with your schedule as a guide. This is easier said than done! All sorts of countervailing forces come up to block us from our most heartfelt intentions. But healing these countervailing forces is the work of the EOL Workshop in general. It is the work of moving out of conflict with our selves and becoming free.

Appendix G

KIDS END OF DAY REVIEW

(CHEAT SHEET)

Step 1. Using your schedule, remember your day.

Step 2. Pause if
1. You felt yukky
2. You didn't do the schedule.
3. You had a tiff with anyone.

Step 3. Process the pause –
1. Change your schedule to fit reality.
2. Honor your want/need to do something by giving it a place on your schedule.
3. Accept that you weren't able to do what you planned because of unforeseen circumstances. Deal with the undone item. Does it need to be done? Decide when you will do it.

4. You didn't feel like it, and you are glad you didn't do it. Deal with whatever is undone and continue your review.

5. You didn't do it, but you wish you did. Identify the motivating voice:
a. Inner Child – identify the need and find a better way to fill it.
b. Inner Parent – identify the belief and see if you agree with it.

6. Negative emotions –
a. Can you prevent it for the future?
b. Name the feeling
c. Sit with the feeling

      i. Notice the feeling sensation of the emotion in your body. Just feel. Don't think.

      ii. Breathe – full belly, full chest, relax, as if you are breathing into the sensation in your body

      iii. Breathe fully while watching any changes in the sensation in your body. Stop when the sensation subsides.

   d. Turn on your brain

      i. Contemplate the problem.

Suggestion list:

   (1) Does this situation come up repeatedly?

   (2) Does this situation/emotion remind you of anything in childhood?

   (3) If the feeling could talk, what words would it be saying? I.e. what beliefs are connected to this feeling? List them. Then for each one think how it *is* true, and think how it *isn't* true. Do you need to recreate your belief? Write it on your MAL or WAL?

   (4) Was the emotion out of proportion to the situation? Possibly a childhood wound?

   (5) Notice what might be the feeling states of the other people involved.

   (6) Ask yourself what they might have been thinking.

   (7) What might have motivated them?

   (8) How might it have felt to them to be on the receiving end of your actions?

   (9) What was motivating you? What did you want/need?

   (10) Can you brainstorm alternative ways you could have acted, and imagine if they might have been more likely to help you reach your goal?

      ii. Decide on a healing course of action

      iii. Put the chosen actions on your calendar, To Do List, schedule, or MAL

7. Tiff with a kid

    a. Consider whether what the child wanted was a need, an OK want, or a not OK want. Become aware of both sides of the issue. Be aware of how the child would be benefited by the granting of the wish, and of what harm it might have caused. If you have difficulty, try the glasses switching exercise on page 142.

    b. Review your words and actions in response to your child.

        i. Were they appropriate to the age of the child (see bicycle analogy)?

        ii. Were they concise and clear, or wishy washy?

        iii. Were they kind or spoken in anger? If you had trouble dealing with your own emotions, try practicing, right now, imaginally, the 'exorcising the demon' exercise on page 107.

    c. If your child is young, review the ICE acronym or the HowToFeelNiceWithAllFolks mnemonic. Might you have taken a different course?

    d. If your child is a teen

        i. Were your interactions parent-child or adult-adult? How would you have spoken about this to an adult renter in your house? Imagine how you could have spoken with respect to your teen. Would you like to apologize?

        ii. Watch your words. Did you use words like allow? must? should? Imagine how you could have spoken giving the reins back to the teen.

        iii. Did you allow your teen to make his own decision (assuming no irreparable harm would take place)?

        iv. Did you take back the reins if irreparable harm was a danger?

        v. Did you put in your two cents?v. Did you put in your two cents?

        vi. Did you support her to learn if she made a mistake?

        vii. Did you act like a doormat, or hold your boundaries by

stating what you will do.

    viii. Or is everything really fine and you just need to have patience?

e. Decide on a healing course of action

f. Put the chosen actions on your calendar, To Do List, schedule or MAL

Step 4. Go back to Step 1. and continue reviewing your day, until you are done.

Step 5. If it is January 1, April 1, July 1, or October 1, then do a Life Review, quickly doing Stage 1, 3 and 4 for each of the 9 areas of life –Body, House, Life's Work, Kids, Life Partner, Community, Emotions, Intellect, Spiritual. Erase any intentions that are no longer needed, brainstorm new intentions as needed, and update your time system.

Appendix H

CHECKING YOUR HOUSE FOR TOXINS

I'm assuming you have a basic understanding of WHY you would want to remove toxins from your home. If not read:

Our Stolen Future by Theo Colburn, et al.
Staying Well in a Toxic World by Lynn Lawson
Is This Your Child's World by Doris Rapp, MD
Chemical Exposures by Ashford and Miller (a difficult read)
Poisoning Our Children by Nancy Sokol Green
Raising Elijah, by Sandra Steingraber

BIG STUFF:

1. Do a radon test
2. Test your water for as much as you can afford. If you have public water, filter it. Drinking out of plastic water containers might not be the wisest choice because of the plastic leaching. Now plastic containers advertise themselves as being BPA free, but the BPA problem was discovered by accident at Tufts University by researchers studying cancer. What about the other chemicals that leach from plastic that weren't found by accident?
4. A Carbon monoxide/smoke alarm is a worthwhile precaution and inexpensive.
5. Be sure your heater is cleaned and maintained twice per year. Call if you (or a friend with a better nose) smells anything when the heat comes on.
6. Running your car in an attached garage fills your house with fumes.

Kids: An Owner's Manual

BEDROOM:

1. You breathe close to your pillow for 1/3 of your life. If you are going to change anything, replace foam pillows with wool ones. Be sure the wool is untreated (just washed). Contact West Earl Knitting Mills (717) 859-2241 for wool, Hobbs (800) 433-3357 for organic cotton and wool batting or you can buy Hobbs on Hancock's of Paducah's internet site, or Harmony catalog for wool pillows (800) 869-3446.

The reason I don't recommend cotton pillows is that unless the cotton is organic, it is sprayed heavily with pesticides. Even if it is organic it will give off "cotton dust." Remember, you don't wash your pillow! Also, cotton will pack after awhile and become uncomfortably dense, whereas wool is very resilient.

2. Replace synthetic sheets with natural fiber sheets. (Wash all clothing/sheets before use. Products have seen a lot of travel before they reach you. If imported they can be sprayed on the boat. They spend time in factories.) Synthetics do offgass to some degree. Since you will be breathing close to your sheets for 8-10 hours per day, the small amount of offgassing becomes more significant.

3. The same logic applies to your mattress. This is a more expensive endeavor so not everyone can afford to replace his synthetic mattresses with an inner spring cotton one. A less expensive option is futon.

Fells Point Futon (410) 563-8866
White Lotus Futon (732) 828-2111 or www.whitelotus.net. Or see other futon web sites.
Custom Bedding - cotton inner spring mattresses and box springs. Crown City Mattress. (818) 796-9101.

4. Carpeting is toxic. The least toxic carpeting I've found is Nature's Carpet. www.colcam.com, or see other web sites.

5. Clothes. When possible buy natural fibers. (Rayon isn't)

PERSONAL HYGIENE:

1. Check for the word "fragrance" on all your toiletries. The word fragrance refers to any combination of 400 different chemicals, one third of which are already known to be toxic.

2. Sodium Lauryl/Laureth Sulfate has been shown to interfere with the development of the retina in young animals. It also exacerbates canker sores. It remains in the body for four days. Most shampoos/toothpastes have it. Giovanni Brand and California Baby Brand shampoos don't. Weleda toothpaste doesn't. Especially keep babies away from it. Speaking of young eyes, there is evidence that it is healthier to have your children sleep in the dark.

3. Hair sprays, gels, dyes, nail polish and remover, etc. are obviously toxic. If you choose to use these, at least ventilate.

4. Try to use deodorant without aluminum chlorohydrate. Try the crystal stick kind.

5. Now that society has finally accepted the germ theory of disease, we are attacking those invisible devils with an Armageddon of toxic weapons. In a vain effort to make our world germ free we are subjecting our own bodies to the same poisons we are using to kill the germs. So don't ignore the downside of germicidal soaps (most notably the new soaps containing Triclosan, which, yes, they sell at the health food store.)

6. Much has been written about fluoride as a toxin. Check the Internet.

7. Bug repellents (OFF and the like) are pesticides. Deet is toxic. Why not just use a citronella or neem based herbal alternative?

CLEANING STUFF:

You can clean your house effectively with just baking soda, vinegar, borax and a few other ingredients. I suggest you obtain <u>Clean and Green</u> by Annie Berthold Bond, or <u>Clean House Clean Planet</u> by Karen Logan.

1. Air fresheners and deodorizers are very toxic. There's lots of proof in the form of dead mice, killed as a service to us by Anderson Labs, the lab that was involved in trying to bring the information about the dangers of carpeting to the public, and was stymied by the EPA, and their buddies the Carpet Lobby. Anderson's website is www.anderson-laboratories.com. Anne Steineman, at the University of Washington, is currently publishing studies about this.

2. Lysol and other commercial disinfectants are similar to pesticides. They are overkill. There are plenty of nontoxic all purpose cleaners in the health food and some grocery stores.

3. Dishwasher detergent and dishwashing liquid, toilet bowl cleaners, furniture polish, oven cleaners, dusting sprays, countertop cleaners, glass cleaners, etc. tend to be quite toxic, but they all have health food store alternatives. Or you can make your own very simply. See books above.

4. Laundry products are particularly important because your family wears the chemicals all day. Most detergents and almost all fabric softeners contain synthetic fragrance (on top of many other toxic compounds) which are toxic.

5. Fabric Softener. This is particularly troublesome for many chemically sensitive people. And if you think of them as canaries in a coal mine, then you'll want to protect your own health by staying away from them too (the fabric softeners, not the canaries). If you use mostly natural fiber clothing, you won't need fabric softener. Some people say

putting vinegar in the rinse cycle helps eliminate static cling.

6. For pest control, consult the Internet. There is a lot of info. Or consult the most commonly used IPM (Integrated Pest Management) manual Common Sense Pest Control by Olkowski et al.

For problems contact NCAMP National Coalition Against the Misuse of Pesticides. (202) 543-5450. www.beyondpesticides.org They are making a list of IPM service providers so you can find one locally.

7. Tile and floors and glass, clean with vinegar. Counters, try Bon Ami. It's like Comet, but nontoxic. Sold in grocery stores. Wood floors, sweep or vacuum. Damp mop. Not too wet though. Dusting, a wet rag is fine.

FOOD:

I think of food as a constant challenge to try to push towards healthy eating. I think, with kids especially, that being too strict about it can be detrimental. I just try to choose healthy options as long as it doesn't freak anyone (including myself) out too much. As far as change goes, slow and steady wins the race. Try to just change one thing at a time and maybe they won't notice!

Things to aim for:

1. Whole foods, as close to their original natural state as possible. Variety is healthful.

2. Avoid additives.

3. Definitely avoid MSG (monosodium glutamate)

4. Avoid food colors.

5. Keep dairy to a minimum. Try to buy dairy labeled "organic" or RBGH free or hormone free. Raw dairy, on the other hand, is quite

healthful.

6. Keep refined sugars to a minimum.

7. If you eat meat, do so in moderation. Especially limit red meat. Organic and grass fed meats are preferable.

8. Organic food is preferable.

9. Many people are wary of the new food invaders - GMO's, soy isolates, and irradiated foods.

10. There is a growing concern about plastics leaching toxic compounds into foods. The softer the plastic the more dangerous. Avoid plastic wrap. Don't cook in plastic - just transfer the frozen food into a glass dish. Store food in glass or stainless steel.

11. Replace your aluminum cookware with stainless steel. Buy baking powder without aluminum.

12. Check out the Internet for info on microwaves.

13. Chlorine bleached (i.e. white) paper products have the danger of dioxin and furon contamination. These are some of the deadliest toxins known to man. This also applies to tampons and pads. Go organic. Go recycled paper. Or check out the Diva cup.

14. Avoid hydrogenated oils.

See HealthyChild.org or EWG.org for more info.

MEDICINE:

1. Learn about alternative medicine. Herbs, homeopathy, nutrition, Chinese medicine, etc. Keep in mind that while modern medicine is a wonderful gift to our society, it is also fueled by big business concerns. The health of the bank accounts of the chemical and drug companies and of the AMA doctors and insurance companies, is often more of a concern in the decisions that are made about your health than is the health of your body.

2. Please read about dental amalgams before allowing another mercury filling in your mouth! ABSOLUTELY only composite fillings should be used on a baby tooth!

OTHER STUFF:

1. Magic Markers, white out, copy machines, paints, give off xylene and other carcinogenic compounds. Keep away from kids. Ventilate.

2. Fluorescent lighting has been shown to be detrimental to human health. If you have fluorescent fixtures at least use full spectrum bulbs.

3. When buying children's toys, look for wood, metal and other natural materials. Avoid or minimize plastics, especially soft plastics (totally avoid plastic teethers) and acrylics.

4. Obviously cotton diapers are preferable to plastic/paper/chemical diapers. Avoid chemical wipes. Even the "alternative" 7th Generation wipes have synthetic fragrance in them. Try bringing little washcloths.

5. You might be surprised at how easily you can create change in your child's school (public and private) by creating a committee to work on an environmental health policy for the school. For support contact the NY Healthy Schools Network.

References

Bailey, B, M.D., (2001). Easy to Love, Difficult to Discipline. New York, NY: William Morrow Paperbacks.

Canfield, D.F. (1986). Her Son's Wife. London, England: Virago Press.

Colborn, T., Myers, J.P., & Dumanoski, D. (1997). Our Stolen Future: Are We Threatening Our Fertility, Intelligence, And Survival?— A Scientific Detective Story. New York, NY: Plume.

Daniels, D., M.D., Marshall, F.G. & Ochberg, F.M. (1970). Violence and the Struggle for Existence. Work of the Committee on Violence of the Department of Psychiatry, Stanford University School of Medicine. Boston, MA: Little Brown & Company.

Gershoff, E.T. (2002). Corporal punishment by parents and associated child behaviors and experiences: A meta-analytic and theoretical review. Psychological Bulletin, 128, 539-579.

Gordon, T. M.D. (2000). Parents Effectiveness Training. New York, NY: Harmony.

Hoffman, E. (1999). A Biography of Abraham Maslow. New York, NY: McGraw-Hill.

Jung, C.G. (1981). The Development of Personality: Papers on Child Psychology, Education, and Related Subjects. Princeton, NJ: Princeton University Press.

Knox & Uvnas-Moberg, (1998). Oxytocin may mediate the benefits of positive social interaction and emotions. Psychoneuroendocrinology Nov, 23 (8), 819-35.

Lawson, L. (1994). Staying Well in a Toxic World: Understanding Environmental Illness, Multiple Chemical Sensitivities, Chemical Injuries, and Sick Building Syndrome. Noble Press.

Liedloff, J. (1986). The Continuum Concept: In Search of Happiness Lost. Cambridge, MA: Da Capo Press.

Lievegoed, B. (2006). Phases of Childhood, Growing in Body Soul and Spirit. Edinburgh, United Kingdom: Floris Books.

Mahdi, L.C., Christopher, N.G., and Meade, M., Eds., (1996). Crossroads: The Quest for Contemporary Rites of Passage. Chicago, IL: Open Court Publishing.

Maslow, A.H., Frager, & R.D., Fadiman, J. (1987). Motivation and Personality. NY, NY: Pearson Education, Inc.

Martin, W. (1999). The Parent's Tao Te Ching: Ancient Advice for Modern Parents. Cambridge, MA: Da Capo Press, a member of the Perseus Books Group.

Nelsen, J. Ed.D. (2006). Positive Discipline. New York, NY: Ballantine Books

Scheer, S. D., Gavazzi, S. M., and Blumenkrantz, D.G. (2007). Rites of Passage During Adolescence. The Forum for Family and Consumer Issues, 12 (2).

Schwartz, E. (2007). Authority and discipline in the life of the child. MillenialChild.com. Retrieved January 15, 2004 from http://millennialchild.com/millennialchild/index.htm

Siegel, D.J., (2015). Brainstorm: The Power and Purpose of the

Teenage Brain., NY,NY: Penguin Publishing.

Tolle, E. (2008). A New Earth: Awakening to Your Life's Purpose. NY, NY: Penguin Publishing Group.

Wachtel, T. (1998). Real Justice. Edinboro, PA: Piper Press.

Weller & Feldman, (2003) Emotion regulation and touch in infants: the role of cholecystokinin and opioids. Peptides May, 24(5), 779-88.

About the Author

Jane Martin, LPC is a psychotherapist in practice at Volition Wellness Center in Skillman, NJ. She is a certified Imago Relationship Counselor and works with many families and children.

She is the founder of Social Harmony, a bullying prevention program for schools – www.SocialHarmonyInstitute.com.

She is co-founder with her daughter Julia, of ReTribe, a Rites of Passage program for teens – www.ReTribe.org.

She trains psychotherapists, with her brother, Ted Riskin, in Breathwork and a ceu program called "Body, Breath, and Spirit in Your Clinical Practice.

And is former owner, with her husband, Dan, of the Natural Baby Company, a leader in the Natural Parenting Movement of the 80s and 90s.

•••